ZAZEN

THE WAY TO AWAKENING

...

story of three zen disciples on their
personal journeys to enlightenment

...

KIDO INOUE

translated by: misako nakatsuka

iUniverse, Inc.
Bloomington

Zazen
The Way to Awakening

iUniverse books may be ordered through booksellers or by contacting:

iUniverse
1663 Liberty Drive
Bloomington, IN 47403
www.iuniverse.com
1-800-Authors (1-800-288-4677)

ISBN: 978-1-4502-7737-2 (sc)
ISBN: 978-1-4502-7739-6 (dj)
ISBN: 978-1-4502-7738-9 (ebook)

Printed in the United States of America

iUniverse rev. date: 02/03/2011

BUDDHA

EN
Calligraphy by Kido Inoue

CONTENTS

...

FOREWORD

In this very busy rhythm of live we have created for ourselves, we forget to see things as for what they are; we sometimes even see more than what things really are.

We let our thoughts, feelings and emotions take over, creating problems throughout our lives that seem impossible to solve stressing about them and in occasions, we simply get lost within.

Practicing Zen will allow you to realize that things are what they are and there is no more than that; what you see is what it is. You come to realize the "Truth" of everything surrounding us and understand that anything beyond is only in your head. With Zen, you are able to recognize and control the occurrence of thoughts, feelings and emotions instead of just regulating them and therefore, truly appreciate your surroundings at total ease. Zen liberates you from your own self letting you to be at "the present moment" where there are no conceptual ideas of the past nor the future as there is neither past nor future existing in the 'now'. You do not stop thinking; you become aware of your thinking process. You do not stop feeling; you simply learn to appreciate more what makes you contempt and purge the feeling that makes you unwove.

This is easily said but not easily done. Because of the already form ideas in our head of everything surrounding us, of everything we see and feel, the guidance and trust of a true Zen Master is imperative. The leadership of a true Zen Master that can direct you to your personal "freedom of the mind" experience is essential. Such leader is Roshi Kido Inoue. His practice is afar from a temple reaching to general public not only within Japan but internationally. Roshi Inoue has given lectures in countries such as Australia, Brazil, France, Iceland, and at institutions like Massachusetts Institute of Technology (MIT) in the United States, among many others. His books have been translated to French and Chinese and now, this is the first book translated to English. He is truly international, proving that anyone who is committed to learn the "Truth" can attain a liberated mind thought the practice of Zen as there is no language barrier to Zen.

In this book you will find the essence of Zen trough the words of Roshi and throughout the experiences of three of his disciples as they describe their first Zen practice.

Please enjoy reading, with an open mind, the experiences of three ordinary individuals and the vast impact that practicing Zen has in their lives.

INTRODUCTION

• • •

- What is Zen? -

Kido Inoue

Zen Buddhism continues to attract worldwide interest. Zen meditation groups are everywhere. This itself is an appropriate and gratifying development. But it is disquieting to acknowledge the origins of this interest in Zen may be due to the ceaseless destruction of the human spirit in today's world and may reflect the yearning for spiritual identity. It may be the expression of people's desire to unleash themselves from the spell of inflated egos.

Progress in material civilization frees people, at least in industrialized economies, from strenuous labor for sheer physical survival. But, it also pampers and traps people in habits of overeating and extravagance, consuming far beyond their real needs. When people's basic needs for survival are met easily, without any compelling effort, they inevitably lose touch with their dynamic sense of being alive in the real world. It is this vitality that gives meaning to hard work, fills the heart with gratitude and joy, and brings contentment to life. This vibrant sense of self evokes the essential goodness of human nature inherent within ourselves. We become capable of appreciating everything we have got, while removing any illusory desire for wasteful consumption.

Humankind has worked hard throughout its history to free itself from the endless struggle to survive and to provide greater material wealth. In that sense, today's world ought to be a dreamland and we should be overjoyed about what we can provide for ourselves. As an old proverb says, "If the body is impoverished, then so is the spirit". However, the Buddha says, "Those who are contented with their life are rich, even if they are poor. Those who are not contented are poor, even if they are rich."

The development of technology has certainly transformed inconveniences to conveniences, discomfort to comfort, and intense perseverance and effort for physical survival are no longer needed. But though we benefit from the development of technology in every sphere of our lives, the pursuit of technological progress is mistaken as the very purpose of humanity.

As a consequence, we are glutted with material things but have lost our sense of gratitude and public moral responsibility. Competition at work is like endless warfare, leaving people stretched to their limits. This is extremely dangerous for our future. Home and school are no longer always nurturing environments for our children. If this trend continues, the damage to our future generations will be irreparable. Underneath the apparently confident appearance of modern men and women lies a profound insecurity and an inability to cope with the desensitizing aspects of this 'high-tech age'. The effect of glorifying technological progress without due care for the spirit is manifested in loss of confidence, absence of appreciation, denigration of altruism and justice, and diminishing social order and communal spirit. The spiritual foundation underpinning the individual - the capacity to empathize and inspire - is being progressively debilitated. Spiritual atrophy is creating serious problems among developed countries.

The awareness of 'our planet earth being a single global village' is potentially enhanced by the information age with its instantaneous transmission of information from one part of globe to the rest of the world. However, peace and progress are hampered largely due to our attachment to egocentric consciousness, self-serving ideologies or dogmatic religions that give no regard to the law of causality. We refuse to see our own part in this, and continually blame others. This low level of spiritual development entrenches people in archaic views of life and stands in the way of spiritual growth and integration. Our minds are polluted by obsolete ideas just as they are polluted by material affluence. And, regrettably, polluted minds keep on polluting many more minds.

As long as humankind lives on this planet applying the current mode of development, then development and destruction will proceed hand in hand. Human dignity, despite our wishes to respect it, will continue to be pushed aside, and our spirituality will continue to wither in our ever more arid inner world. When our mind is out of balance, we lose confidence. We find harder to connect with other people, let alone trust, respect, and appreciate them. We lose touch with the goodness of our human nature. Under such circumstances, it is impossible to expect our actions to reflect truth, goodness, beauty, love, courage, and justice. These are qualities essential for living together in harmony. Without them, our life is tossed about by rampant egoism and endless conflicts. Such peaceful coexistence can grow only when mutually giving and receiving peace and joy becomes the essential focus of our life. However, if our spirit is already damaged, it is inconceivable that we can be genuinely concerned with the well-being of other people. And it is the damaged spirit that gives rise to every human evil on this earth.

I have named this phenomenon 'the developmental desensitization syndrome.' It has already spread around the world like a chronic disease. Its consequences are ominous as they are the manifestation of core problems in our inner world that neither the political nor educational system can resolve. That is why the restoration and enhancement of the spirit must be given the greatest priority in life. This must outweigh cultural and educational activities, because without spirit, it is impossible to achieve the full potential of a vibrant and healthy global community. Without spiritual redemption, there is no lasting peace of mind.

A clouded spirit is the direct consequence of egoism running amok which only swamps us with mumyo, or spiritual ignorance, and suffering. Those who became aware of this often turn to religion for an answer. Zen practice offers a way in which people can address the inevitable drama of life as a positive challenge and live everyday life with satisfaction and a sense of direction.

The ultimate aim of Zen is to break out of the constraints of ego and have direct personal experience of the absolute infinity of our being. It is to awaken to the truth of our nature beyond the ego. In a nutshell, Zen focuses on the essence of mind.

The human mind is inherently free. It neither affirms nor denies. It is not constrained by the conflict of the opposites, like right and wrong or self and others. An awakened mind knows that the dynamic unity between self and others forms part of an integrated whole. Having direct knowledge of this mind brings profound peace. The teachings of the Buddha point the way to acquire this knowledge through direct personal experience.

As Dogen, the great Zen master, put it, "Zazen is our practice to experience the truth, and that practice itself is the truth." Serious Zen practice purifies the mind; as the mind settles down, a glimpse of the truth unfolds spontaneously.

Zen practice aims at attaining unity with being. When the false boundary that separates mind and body from the universe dissolves, and the self is perceived to be a part of the whole, one can break away from the very source of false attachments, false fear, and false thinking. This is the liberation of mind; the mind is awakened to see the essence of the real world. This awakened mind is what we call the enlightened mind. Free from false fear and attachments, the enlightened mind is filled with compassion, appreciation, and contentment.

What is Zen? How relevant is the Buddha's teaching for oneself? How does Zen help function in everyday life? Is enlightenment attainable? If so, what are the steps to get there? What to focus one self's attention on? What happens when one commits oneself to practice?

These are the questions anyone aspiring to practice Zen first asks. Unfortunately, the guidance available in Japan as well as the rest of the world today does not always fully respond to these questions nor enable students to experience the benefits of practice. Unless teachers are capable of offering clear-cut guidance, in understandable language, the students' dedication and commitment may result in even greater confusion.

Before starting to read this book, I would ask the reader to 'just read,' without attachment to any preconceived notion of Zen. I also need to warn the reader that to expect that you can understand Zen through a little reading is a complete illusion, and your complacency will be nothing but a barrier to your growth. Zen starts to unfold only when thought is consciously abandoned, and there is no more conscious mind. This book is designed to provide the reader with a few landmarks and a practical methodology for treading the path of Zen. There is a huge gap between intellectual understanding and embodying understanding through direct experience. The scope of intellectual understanding is acutely limited. In order to grasp the Original Self, a Zen student must meditate to push beyond the limits of the intellect.

As Dogen put it, "Without zazen, practicing Zen is never authentic. Likewise, without zazen, enlightenment is never authentic."

The liberation of each individual mind from the small self is what truly counts and is the only effective way to eventually resolve the conflicts, anguish and suffering confronting the world and humankind. We need to be acutely aware that we cannot count on anything other than the collective effort of liberated individuals and the law of causality in creating a better world for our future generations.

Kido Inoue
15 November 1987.

MY SEARCH FOR SELF-LIBERATION

• • •

BY: HISANORI JYURAKU

MY SEARCH FOR SELF-LIBERATION

• • •

Hisanori Jyuraku
High school teacher / born in 1942

I was forty years old, and a high school teacher, when I first stepped into the Zen temple, Kaizoji, one summer holiday. The students' photography club, to which I was an adviser, had organized a summer workshop at Kaizoji. One of the club members happened to be the daughter of the Zen master who had made the temple available for the workshop. This was how my first encounter with Zen began.

Until that time, not only had I no interest in religion, rather, I believed religion could have a poisoning effect like drugs, inviting anti-social behavior, and misleading people who are incapable of rational thinking. Though my impression of Zen was vague, it did not quite fall into the category of such religions.

Thus, one hot summer night, I sat meditating for the first time in my life with my students in this small Zen temple. I was slightly nervous. Burning incense, combined with the dim candlelight illuminating the Buddha statue, created a religious atmosphere.

Our Roshi, or Zen teacher, looked relatively young, perhaps in his early forties. Wearing luminous white robes overlaid with a diaphanous black robe, he spoke with that fullness of spirit that can come only from someone who knows from personal experience what he is talking about. It was a refreshing experience and left me with a sense of peace, although I could not comprehend many of the things he touched on. They were way beyond what we usually talk about in daily life.

Roshi said, "The whole purpose of zazen is 'just sitting'. You focus on your being, just sitting in this very moment. Zazen is a practice to become awakened as your Original Self. It is through this awareness that you see truth, hear truth, and think truth; in other words, you embrace life as it truly is. There is an oneness between your Original Self and truth. The Original Self is free from vanity, malice, hypocrisy, lust and self-pity. This is the path of self-liberation and enlightenment. Since ancient times, thousands of path-seekers have dedicated their lives to finding their Original Self. This search is the most rewarding pursuit there is. Up to now you might not have been fully aware of the Original Self within yourself, but now you can know its presence. Start your practice right this moment. Apply yourself to find this Original Self through becoming one with your breathing. Forget yourself through being totally in the moment."

As Roshi revealed the essence of Zen to me for the first time, I understood far more clearly why I had this vague impression that Zen did not quite fit into the ordinary category of religion. Roshi gave us a technique for sitting, or zazen. "The key to experiencing no-self is to be one with each inhalation and exhalation. If you can do this, you can penetrate the root of all your suffering." Following his instruction, I made an all-out effort to sit.

It dawned on me much later that even though I thought I was doing zazen with determination, my effort was inconsequential. My mind kept spinning with busy thoughts. Time went by extremely slowly because my mind was restless. I tried to concentrate on breathing, but not a single breath was free from thoughts. The restlessness of my mind was not because of zazen it happened all the time in daily life.

After the meditation, I purposely did not set time aside with my students to discuss their impression of zazen, although this would usually be beneficial. But I thought it would be better for them to keep their experiences at the temple to themselves.

A few days later, I visited Kaizoji with my high-school colleague, Mr. Waki, to thank Roshi for his assistance during the workshop. Roshi introduced us to Mr. Kozumi, who also happened to be visiting. Mr. Kozumi sat with a beautiful straight posture, and spoke clearly and confidently about his recent experience of sesshin, an intensive schedule of zazen and physical work. He impressed me as a vivacious, good man. He told us he had only just reached the gateway to Zen; he described the unfolding process of his mind during zazen, the bliss and wonder of being in the moment. "At times I thought I might go mad. Here I was stepping into a totally unknown world all alone. I was visited by delusion after delusion. In the end, I no longer knew who I was. I had no choice but to believe in Roshi's words and keep on trying 'to be one with my breathing.' In my business I almost went bankrupt twice, but I tell you, it was nothing compared with the agony I went through in zazen." Mr. Kozumi was very open about the most trying moments of his practice, so I could see how zazen had demanded that he go beyond his limits. I was enthralled by this insight into Zen practice. It opened up a new world for me.

Mr. Kozumi's sincere respect for Roshi was evident in his every gesture and word, quite different from cosmetic politeness or courtesy. In his forties, he was at the peak of his business career, a competent man with a high social profile. I said to myself, 'What was it that turned Mr. Kozumi on?' If what I was observing was authentic, Roshi must surely have some astounding quality to attract respect from people. Still, I was not sure what was so special about him.

Mr. Kozumi's direct experience of zazen was so convincing that I no longer had any excuse to run away from Zen. So, I made a decision on the spot to practice zazen. As I reflect now, it was Mr. Kozumi's enthusiasm and self-assurance that gave me the courage to overcome my anxiety; without him, I do not think I could have been so decisive. It is wonderful how a personal encounter can act as a catalyst to spark off experiences totally beyond one's imagination.

Roshi said, "If you want zazen for a hobby, you had better go somewhere else. If you come to me, you had better be serious and ready to meditate around the clock."

According to Mr. Kozumi, "The first three days were hell; I wept every day. It was too painful. Frankly I wished someone could have sent me a fake telegram saying that a member of my family had died, and that I needed to leave this place."

These comments made me nervous. Could I endure sesshin? But now that the date was set between the seventeenth and twenty-fourth of August, I did not want to stop halfway. I wanted to get something out of this experience.

I started to practice zazen at home, as I still had a week before the sesshin. I tried to focus my mind on a single point, thus hopefully avoiding any diffusion of attention. I tried, as advised by Roshi, to concentrate on this very moment of inhalation and exhalation and hold on to it. I tried in vain. Still, one hour of zazen was refreshing.

My wife and two children were baffled; they must have sensed the intense energy around me when I was meditating, but they seemed to respect the space I needed.

First Day

On the seventeenth of August at 1:00 p.m. I arrived at Kaizoji. Roshi and Kaizoji are there to guide people on the path. I, too, was coming to this temple for the single purpose of finding my Original Self. I braced myself for the journey.

As usual, Roshi served a cup of green tea when I arrived.

Although it was a hot day, I did not feel the heat. There was neither noise nor tranquility. The only thing I felt was this indefinable tension about setting out into an unknown world. I was the only one in the zendo. Roshi looked at me with piercing eyes, and spoke with tremendous passion and energy about the purpose of zazen and the way to practice it.

"The purpose of zazen is enlightenment. Enlightenment is attaining true liberation of mind by removing blockages. Life reveals its meaning when one can act in harmony with the truth and gain deep satisfaction from it. Life is not worthwhile if one cannot act in harmony with the truth and gain true satisfaction from it.

What blocks the mind? Blockages are your ego, your superiority or inferiority complex, your false self-image, opinions, and the ideas you are holding onto. They affect your perception; they hamper you from experiencing this immediate present and living in its fullness. These blockages will trip you up anytime. Do not allow any space for them. Concentrate on the moment in your zazen, and you will eventually surrender your body and mind and fuse with the experience of zazen. Where are your blockages then? They are all gone.

What is the practice for if you come out of darkness and go back into darkness again? Practice without strong aspiration will not endow you with the spiritual strength to stem the roots of your attachments and often ends up in the mere pursuit of a cosmetic lifestyle. Above anything else, you must work on your spiritual salvation first. Focus on attaining and then sustaining a state of mind without any thoughts, fantasies, or needs. Zen practice asks you to be totally focused in each moment, whatever you do. Do not divert your attention from what you are doing, be it sitting, standing, walking or sleeping. Train yourself to just be the moment with the precision of one-hundredth of a second. When you learn to focus on one breath, then the next breath and the next, your busy mind will start to quiet down, and eventually you can simply be in whatever you do, moment by moment. When you leave reasoning behind and are at ease with the very moment, the Original Self starts to emerge. This Original Self is free and spontaneous without any restraints. Be absolutely serious and concentrate on each breath. In the end, it becomes clear that there is nothing else other than the present moment.

When your feet are hurting, change your zazen position. When you cannot resist dozing off, have a sleep. If you are strongly committed to seek your Original Self, you will wake up refreshed after sleep. Apply yourself. Make an all-out effort."

His guidance was thorough, though I only came to appreciate Roshi's teaching capacity much later. Roshi is capable of empowering any student to step onto the path of Zen as long as the student trusts him and practices under his guidance.

I thought I had full trust in Roshi and accepted his guidance without any hesitation. In retrospect, I must admit I only listened to and accepted a fraction of Roshi's teachings, let alone understood them. What I thought I understood at that time had either the wrong focus, was too superficial, or was a gross misinterpretation. In short, I was screening his teaching through my own preconceived ideas and listened only to what I wanted to hear.

Following his instruction, I wore kimono and hakama, a pleated skirt for kimono; this made me feel more inspired to start zazen. Worldly desires, attachments, and sloth already seemed remote.

"There might be some visitors coming into the zendo. You can politely ignore them and concentrate all your attention so you do not get distracted." Having said that, Roshi disappeared. I was left feeling both abandoned and relieved at the same time.

I was not ready to start zazen right away. I walked around on the tatami mat and then lay down. I was waiting for something to happen next, just like being on a train and waiting for it to leave the station. About thirty minutes went idly by. I grew increasingly unsettled.

The moment I stepped into the zendo, I should have started zazen immediately. In reality, I wasted thirty minutes till enough tension rose to push myself into doing what I had come here for. This was pathetic. Unless I grew out of this slackness, there was no way I would find my Original Self and live an enhanced life.

At last I was ready to apply myself seriously. I lit a stick of incense and sat right in front of the Buddha statue. Initially I tried to place my attention on the breath passing through my throat; then I remembered that Roshi did not recommend this. So I tried to focus my attention on breathing and breathing only. Concentration on the moment was not easy. My mind drifted away, and thoughts started to run amok. Even worse, I got caught up in them and it took me a long while to realize my lapses in attention. I kept telling myself, 'Go back to the present moment. Concentrate on breathing', but soon my mind was distracted again. The process of bringing my attention back to the breathing was repeated endlessly.

The fact was that nothing helped bring the present moment under control.

Willpower, aspiration, resolution, knowledge, all these things I should have been able to count on, had no direct impact. In spite of my meticulous effort, my mind could not stay with 'just breathing' even for a second. I knew this stage full well through my preliminary practice at home. All beginners go through this stage; so I did not have to be disappointed with my performance. The first day had gone by without my getting the knack of zazen. I woke up frequently that night; I could not sleep well.

Second Day

I woke up charged at 4:00 a.m., and this time was ready to do zazen. My pursuit of the present moment seemed more smooth this morning. While I was more poised, incoherent thought after thought kept raging through my mind with great vigor. Not only did they emerge, but I almost drowned in them. Thoughts kept attacking me with their kaleidoscopic forms and appearances, leaving me not even a moment for a breathing spell. Desire and emotions took control of my mind completely. I could appreciate how Zen practice at this stage was a battle; my mind would either fall prey to illusory thoughts and emotions or it would stand firm and fight them off to establish a sense of my Original Self.

"Remember Zen practice is geared to focus the mind in the present moment." Roshi's words were an illuminating guidepost, pointing in the right direction. I kept them close to my heart to bring my attention back to just breathing, here and now. Had I not had his words as a reminder, I do not think I would have even noticed my mind was being distracted by thoughts and emotions.

Roshi seemed to know exactly when to turn up in the zendo. I was starting to feel weary, and there he was to give me some encouragement. "You must never ever back off in the struggle against attachments to the small self. You must be in power instead of letting them control you. Otherwise, practicing zazen means nothing. Practice being the present moment completely. The present moment is eternity. All we have forever is this very moment; thus, eternity is made up of now and only now. This immediate moment is clearly distinct from the immediate past and future. However, when the boundary between them is blurred, you are blocked from your Original Self. Drop the past and future; rid yourself even of the immediate past and future. Then the Original Self unfolds and can fully function in the present so that whatever you are doing, you can be totally mindful. The Original Self is without any confusion and self-doubt; it leaves no space for anything but meticulous attention to the present moment.

We get so caught up with our attachments to memory, opinions and judgments that we can no longer distinguish our entangled mind from the Original Self, and we suffer with our own delusions, clouding the clarity of just being here and now. This happens all the time; when it does, go back immediately to focus your mind on the moment, through your breath, and thus sever any thoughts of the past and future. Direct experience of the present lifts you beyond suffering, and your mind is restored to its original freedom and luminosity."

Roshi kept giving me encouraging suggestions to bring my mind back to the present; his remarks motivated me to apply myself harder. To be honest, I could never have imagined that just being in the present could be so difficult. It was an insurmountable challenge to go beyond noisy thoughts; thoughts continued to rush through my mind. I was out of sorts, disappointed, and ready to quit. Somehow, I managed to hang in there. With my mind quieting down, I became more aware of each physical movement I made. I was also more aware of the loving care of Roshi's wife in preparing each meal, and was able to feel that her food was nourishing my life.

The toilet happened to be at the corner of the main hall. I had to pass by Roshi's room to get there. As I walked along the corridor, I concentrated on each step, leaving no space for thoughts to sneak in. Still, Roshi shouted at me from his open room. "You are not being mindful with your steps. Pay a hundred times more attention to each step!"

The moment he shouted, I focused all my attention and checked whether I was 'just walking.' To my frustration, there was always room for more concentration. How could he shout at me and tell me the same thing over and over again at exactly the same spot? If he had not pulled me up, I would not have known. I would have remained complacent, thinking this was my best effort. Only when told could I realize that my focus was still diffuse and remote from the reality of 'just walking.' It was annoying to think Roshi only had to glance at me walking along the corridor to know the state of my mind. I could not evoke extraordinary concentration and stillness of mind all on my own; perhaps this is one of the reasons students must have Zen teachers to guide them. In simple movements like walking, I was completely lost as to what I should be focusing my attention on. In order to walk, hands and legs move simultaneously. Accordingly, not just the whole body, but whatever comes into vision also keeps moving.

What did Roshi mean by 'just be and walk,' while there were so many movements that involve walking? I had not the slightest idea exactly which part of my walking movements I ought to concentrate on. Roshi had said, "When walking, just walk, leaving no space for thoughts to sneak in. Put yourself in that one step completely." But how could I apply myself completely while I was engrossed in the details of what made up each step? It seemed the only way I could find the answer was to keep trying to focus on each step. There was immense tension between the mind that wanted to run away and the mind that was determined to focus on each step.

Even when I was on the toilet, I wondered what to center my mind on, because unless my mind was fixed on something, it was immediately swept away with endless thoughts. And, when it ran rampant, it tended to remain agitated, forever disrupting the sense of centeredness. Unless I could bring this mind habit under control, there would be no progress. As I understand it, Zen practice opens the way to return to the Original Self, an authentic, luminous existence. The Original Self is free from any craving for recognition; it is happy to give credit to others for its achievement. The Original Self is content to take life on its own terms; it lives in total dedication to the relationship it forms here and now. However, our small self perpetually blocks the awareness of the Original Self. Or, to put it another way, the small self is the very source of distractions that defy the presence of the Original Self, not taking what we are seriously. If I gave up zazen, and quit this quest for my Original Self, I would be forever stuck with my small self. Unless I could just be this very moment, free from the past and future, I could not live as my Original Self. As long as my mind was trapped in its habitual spinning, there was no sense of centeredness, no access to my essence. Above anything else, I needed to quieten my turbulent mind. Although I tried to apply myself more consistently, there was no progress on the second day. At best, I was slightly more settled. Was I lacking in effort? Was I ill-focused? Or was I not suited to zazen? My whole body was stiff and aching. I was exhausted, and felt barren and miserable. I could not bear it anymore. Tears kept rolling down my cheeks and I wondered if tears ever helped to prepare the ground for self-transformation.

Third Day

Had I slept at all during the night? When I noticed I was already doing zazen at dawn, it seemed that my body had moved of its own volition. The room was still dim. The small light of an incense stick looked much bigger than I thought it was.

I wanted to leave this place as soon as possible. Spinning thoughts, whirling thoughts assailed me with growing intensity. But it was too early to quit! It was only the third day. I thought to myself what else could I expect to attain in life if I gave up on zazen on the third day? Stay with it. I might be on the verge of clearing the first hurdle.

With renewed determination, I mustered all my vital energy and kept on practicing zazen. It was my firmest intention ever.

And it made a wonderful difference. I could let go of noisy thoughts with greater ease and bring my mind back to concentrate on my breath. I could observe a single breath with much more clarity and precision. What Roshi had been trying to teach me yesterday suddenly rang a bell.

He had said, "You start breathing in, continue to breathe in, and finish breathing in. Then you must clearly acknowledge in your mind that the inhalation is complete. And together with that awareness, shed all thoughts and emotion. Leave them all behind. Your mind is cleaned up with nothing to hold on to. In this state of nothingness just breathe out quietly. Breathe out thoroughly. Then just breathe in. Breathe in thoroughly. Practice with single-minded concentration. When the mind-noise starts, use breathing to let it go and just be the present moment."

At last his instructions made sense. Being fully determined to have another go, I breathed with the utmost care and stillness. I was breathing in. I was breathing out. Then breathing in and breathing out. Great! I could breathe naturally without any difficulty. It was incredibly easy.

The mind-noise appeared and disappeared like flashes on a screen. But I could watch it coming and going from a distance, remaining totally detached. It was no longer obstreperous. I didn't have to fight, but simply let my mind flow with the breath. My mind could stay focused on each inhalation and exhalation, although not for long.

It was completely different from 'concentration' in the ordinary sense. It was 'mindless mindfulness.' This was a major breakthrough. I could let the breath guide me, instead of struggling with thoughts. As usual, Roshi came into the hall unexpectedly. Almost as an automatic response, I straightened my spine. I was apprehensive. I had no idea what he was seeing in me.

He sat in front of me face to face and abruptly asked, "What is walking?"

It was self-explanatory. "Walking is taking steps forward."

"No!"

"It is to step forward by moving alternate legs."

"No!"

What did Roshi want me to say? "Walking is mu, or freedom without any restriction."

"No, don't ruin your mind with concepts. You have been walking all your life and you mean you still have not figured out what walking is about? Tell me! Tell me what walking is!"

With glaring eyes he shouted and drew even closer to me. I was utterly confused and embarrassed, and lost for words.

"You will never understand walking by analyzing and theorizing about it. Concepts must be given up!"

Suddenly Roshi slapped me on my cheek. "Tell me, what is walking!"

My mind went blank. I was disoriented. I could not think straight. I lost my sense of who I was. It was as if I was floating in the air, weightless, without any resistance of body and mind. All the tension was gone. Without any thought I stood up and started walking. It was an unconscious move, but the moment I walked I was convinced, 'This is it. There is no other answer.'

"You've got it at last! That is what walking is about. All of your descriptions are merely images of walking and have nothing to do with the reality of walking. When you focus on images, you lose sight of the simplest reality, such as walking. There is nothing other than reality. Reasoning is useless in the face of reality. The intellectualizing process does not own the reality of walking."

Roshi's words were unraveling my self-entangling thought processes. Now he challenged me with another question. "What is sitting?"

Only a few seconds ago, I had grasped the reality of walking. I knew all I needed to do was to simply sit without any explanation. So I sat spontaneously.

"If you do not resort to reasoning, reality is manifested 'as it is', in its fullness. And that is all there is. Nothing special."

The moment I heard this, I felt as if a curtain had risen. This time I was able to share the depth of his words. I nodded with profound agreement. Just walking or sitting without any thoughts brought me back to the total spontaneity and innocence of a baby.

"Reality is just doing what you are doing in the present moment. You must be devoid of interpretations; rather let the reality of each moment manifest itself. Zen is a discipline to drop the self and be wholly present. And by so practicing you cut off the roots of delusions, attachments, and false thinking, you forget yourself utterly and completely. Your Original Self will then unfold and teach you. This is the state of satori or enlightenment in which the mind is freed from delusions. This is Buddhahood. Someone who has actually got hold of the suchness of the present moment through direct personal experience is a truly awakened person. However, the moment the mind is distracted from just being, Buddhahood eludes you, and you are one billion light-years away from the enlightened state. When you strive and practice to be awake in the moment, your meticulous attention brings you back to Buddhahood and fills you with the luminosity of the Buddha."

Roshi was sharing the essence of the Buddha's teaching, and I felt convinced for the first time that they could lead to radical liberation. Once again, I felt fortunate to have Roshi as my teacher and guide and renewed my great respect for him. Mr. Kozumi was right. Now I understood what he had been talking about.

The reality of the present moment was right here within my reach when I dropped everything, thoughts, opinions, reasons, and judgments. My sense of despair and failure transformed into relief, fulfillment and stupendous joy. Roshi and I looked at each other and burst out laughing, genuine, spontaneous laughter from the belly.

I rang up Mr. Kozumi immediately. As if he was waiting for my phone call, he asked, "Have you got hold of the present moment?"

I said, "Yes!" again with happy laughter.

Then I was allowed to clean the hall for the first time. 'What a blissful state of mind!' I said to myself as I started cleaning.

As usual Roshi appeared out of nowhere. "What is the purpose of cleaning?" he asked abruptly.

Knowing he accepted no explanation, I simply said, "It is to keep the place neat and tidy."

"Yes, you are right. But once you start cleaning, are you still reminding yourself of your intention to clean up?"

"No, I am not."

"Why not?"

I was stuck for words. Then I said, "Because I am focused on just cleaning."

"Exactly. The intention to clean is an aspiration. It directs your energy to achieve a desired goal. But once you start, there is simply doing. You don't need to keep thinking about it because you are already doing it. Most people mix up intention with practice. The time when you thought about your intention and the time when you translated your intention into action are not the same. Yet the distinction is not clear; therefore you cannot completely engage yourself in what you are doing. Let me ask you, what is cleaning?"

In response, I simply swept the floor with the broom I held. It was remarkable. I wasn't even thinking. But I had a gut feeling that sweeping was absolutely the only thing I needed to do.

"Fine. Then how many times do you need to sweep to finish the cleaning?"

Again I tried not to analyze. This time I didn't know what to do. I faltered. I tilted my head slightly in embarrassment. Suddenly Roshi slapped me. It was amazingly quick. I became more anxious to find an answer but I knew full well that giving him an estimate would not do. The answer must have something to do with practicing moment by moment. But what was it?

"When do you sweep?" Roshi asked.

"Now."
"How many times can you sweep now?"

"Once."
Oh! Yes, it had clicked at last. Because my mind had been caught up in figuring how many times I would need to sweep to finish, I failed to realize the whole process was made up of what I did each moment. Each moment right here and right now is the only time I have. It is the absolute moment, without past or future. As long as I am totally engaged with what I am doing right now, there is no room for false thinking and suffering.

Roshi left saying, "What is truly real, right in this moment, is the single act of sweeping. Just be totally mindful in each act of sweeping."

I continued to sweep and then began to mop the hall. I mopped slowly and meticulously. It must have been a fair amount of time but it went like a flash. There was an incredible quality of clarity as if I had direct access to the universe and the universe was working through me. I wrung the cloth in total stillness; with it, I mopped the floor from left to right and right to left. It was a deeply purifying and refreshing act. After cleaning the whole place, I stood there, taking stock of myself. To my surprise, there was no trace of 'I-am-ness' or what 'I' had attained. This must be what Roshi described as 'emptiness at work.' I would not have had the nerve to claim that I had experienced a state of complete emptiness; but at least I was convinced that when the mind gives total attention to 16 whatever one is doing, there is no longer any separation between the self and the activity.

I put all the cleaning gear back into place. While washing my hands, I casually glanced out the window at the ocean. It was stunningly beautiful. Could it be the same landscape I had been seeing for the past forty years? Now I understood what Mr. Kozumi meant when he said, "You start seeing things as they are, in their absolute glory, as your mind gets clearer." All these years I had not been really seeing. Now everything around me was intimate because I could experience its full presence without analyzing, interpreting and judging. It was seeing the essence of things beyond the level of consciousness. As Roshi put it, "When you can just let yourself be, you and the universe are an inseparable part of the whole." Yes, that is exactly what I was experiencing. How liberating to be in the present. Breathing was surprisingly easy. Previously, each breath had been heavy and uncontrollable simply because I had no feel for being one with the moment. The reality was nothing complex, just simple breathing. Whatever I was doing, scrubbing, sweeping, or walking, I was touching the same truth as long as I was solely concerned with the present moment. I was thrilled with this insight. Then I saw Mr. Kozumi walking into the zendo. With total spontaneity we bowed with our hands on the tatami floor, a gesture only done on special formal occasions.

"Congratulations!" he said.

"Thank you," I said, and really meant it.

My guard had dropped, and I felt much closer to Mr. Kozumi. I was delighted with his friendship, his coming to congratulate me on gaining a glimpse of being in the moment. Perhaps because my mind was less blocked, I felt a spiritual connection to him, my co-traveller on the Zen path. Our minds were much richer and bigger than I had ever imagined. I was glad that I had persisted.

Roshi came in with his wife. She bowed politely and gave me warm congratulations. I could genuinely express my gratitude to her for her support. Everyone looked so radiant and beautiful. I was filled again with laughter and we all joined in a great roar.

That was the best celebration ever. While drinking sake, we shared our Zen experiences on the sunny verandah. From our conversation it became clear that Roshi's wife also had direct knowledge of Zen. No wonder she struck me as having an extraordinary quality while doing ordinary things.

Roshi said, "Mr. Jyuraku, you have only reached the gateway to the Zen path. Don't be too pleased with your progress. Previously you had not the slightest idea of how to practice zazen, whereas now you have an inkling. To tell you the truth, even reaching the level you have is extremely difficult. If students start from the wrong path, they could spend forty or fifty years without getting anywhere."

I did not care if it was just the gateway. To me the difference was like night and day. I was absolutely exhilarated and also knew I could never have reached it had I not met Roshi. Most people, including myself, tend to think we know ourselves best. The truth is, once we step into our inner world, what unfolds there is quite unlike how we thought we were. It is like walking into a dark jungle of confusing thoughts, illusion and fantasy. The right teacher provides a map and a torch. With extraordinary alertness, a Zen master can read from the tiniest gesture where a student is at, what he is confused about, where he is about to go, and what guidance needs to be given.

Tranquility returned after Roshi's wife and Mr. Kozumi left.

Seeing me on top of the world, Roshi warned me to stay focused. "Mr. Jyuraku, the state of mind you are in does not yet have sustaining power and will not give you lasting inner strength in life. The noises of your mind have quieted down, just as dirt sinks to the bottom of water. But once you are exposed to the hustle and bustle of everyday life, your mind will immediately lose its stillness, like dirt being stirred up. You are only at the gateway to the path, the starting point for real Zen training. So there is no time for complacency. Keep up your yearning for the path."

Roshi made me feel the time I had left was extremely precious. I returned to the zendo immediately and continued zazen. My mind retained the same stillness as before. I had clear awareness of being in the present. My thoughts had almost receded, and in between were moments of none at all. If they did emerge, I could readily let them go and return to the present.

In the afternoon, I had permission to sweep the garden. I could totally immerse myself sweeping with a broom from side to side. There was no 'I-am-ness' trying to achieve something; the whole process was blissful.

The third day marked a milestone for me. I was able to act with the total spontaneity of a baby, which then opened up a world free from any thoughts, judgments, and opinions. I felt deep appreciation to Roshi for the experience, and went to sleep in peace.

Fourth Day

I woke up completely refreshed. It was 4:00 a.m. and I started to practice zazen immediately. After a while I suddenly knew that another layer of personal barriers had dropped away. This gave me a sense of intimacy and intervening with everything that surrounded me. It was a cataclysmic change that happened in a flash. I did not have any overwhelming emotion but felt lighter and grounded at the same time. Doing zazen was no longer a gruesome effort.

Drinking the mugicha, (wheat tea), Roshi's wife had left for me; I could appreciate it with total mindfulness. My whole being was committed to the moment, just drinking tea. Now it was crystal clear to me that, as this rigid self-fades away, we make space available to illuminate the Original Self that is free and spontaneous.

Roshi gave me forewarning that I should expect some breakthrough and, if that happened, I should come to him immediately. I could not wait to see him, and rushed to his room. Even before I started, he said "So, a new development." I told him of my experience of intervening with my surroundings.

Then Roshi knocked the desk and asked, "What is this?"

With total spontaneity, I knocked the desk the same way as Roshi and said, "This is it."

Without a pause, Roshi picked up a glass and asked, "What is this?"

Amazing! I understood the gist of his questions with great ease when my mind was 'emptied,' with nothing to take hold of. Usually, when we gain knowledge or form an opinion about something, we examine it as an object, as something or someone to understand. By doing so, we create a separation of subject from object and block ourselves from fully knowing what it is, 'as it is'. As soon as 'it' is identified and defined by the intellect, the artificial maneuver of 'it' is underway. However, we are mistakenly led to believe that limited definitions represent 'it' in its totality.

In truth, to know anything in its wholeness, we need to first let preconceived notions and emotions go; we cannot do this without breaking through the limited confines of the small self. The mind, when focused on the here-and -now, is available to let the 'what is' speak to us. Roshi was there to guide us to experience the wholeness of what is, 'as it is'. That was why he repeatedly challenged us to make sure our understanding was in our bones, not just our heads.

"I can see you are more at peace with yourself," said Roshi.

Yes, I was blissful; it was as if there was nothing to hold onto, and yet I was blessed with abundance. It was much more than gaining stillness of mind; a totally new vista suddenly opened up with vivid intensity. Roshi looked pleased with the process I was going through.

"Let's take a bath," he said, out of the blue.

It was my first bath since I had come here. The bathroom was spacious enough for two people.
While I was scrubbing my back, Roshi abruptly shouted, "What are you doing now?"

With Roshi one cannot slacken even for one instant. "I am doing this," I answered, without stopping scrubbing my back with vigor.

"Why are you doing this?" Roshi pressed me further.

"Because this is this. There is nothing else other than this," said I, still scrubbing my back.

Roshi came right in front of me and this time stuck his hand out deliberately. "Do you see what I mean?"

Then he turned his hand and showed me its back. If Roshi had done this to me the previous day, I would have been distracted, could not have controlled my thoughts and been totally flustered. However, today I no longer needed any words to respond to him.
Roshi continued. "Be 'as it is'. Just be."

His words calmed me and made me feel even more grounded. It was my most valuable practice experience so far. Roshi seemed to know exactly when to create triggers to help me break through reason and move into a state of transparency.
After taking our bath, we sat together at the small table, enjoying the breeze of an electric fan. Watching Roshi quietly serving tea for me, I realized

there was no boundary between us; his flowing movements felt like my own. This, I thought, must be what Buddhists call jita-ichinyo, or unity of self and others. Clearly, Roshi and I were present as two individuals, but our beings were so blended in harmony that there was no separation of myself from his self. There was not even any space left for me to be grateful to Roshi for the experience he was guiding me through. 'I-am-ness' dissolved; so did Roshi as a separate identity.

I drank my tea with natural elegance, sitting up straight and holding the teacup with both hands, as in the Japanese tea ceremony. But why was this happening with no effort? I had never practiced tea ceremony in my life. Was it because, as the mind grew purer and more in harmony with beauty, anything I did mirrored that state of mind?

Throughout zazen the focus of my attention was on my mind; I had never thought that zazen would visibly affect my external behavior. Now I realized I was more mindful of the way I talked, walked, or sat; my posture had improved enormously and, with my mental blocks dissolving, my face looked alight. Readers might laugh if I said I even looked more dignified when I saw myself in the bathroom mirror.

Now I understood why Mr. Kozumi always drank tea so gracefully. 'Why bother with the onerous manners of the tea ceremony?' used to be my attitude. But now it was clear to me that the crux of the tea ceremony was 'being fully in the moment.'

Afterwards, whatever I did seemed to flow naturally. Walking to the bathroom, I saw across the corridor the tiny backyard covered with fallen leaves. Previously this backyard had looked cluttered, and the leaves messy. Now, the same fallen leaves gave me a totally different impression; they were neither making this place messy nor adorned; by the same token, they were neither dispensable nor indispensable. Their stunning beauty did not leave room for any duality. I was thrilled by the profound and subtle colors of the withered leaves, the multiplicity of their unique shapes, and the random yet perfect arrangement of those leaves on the ground. Their beauty was breathtaking. In that instance I needed nothing beyond this beauty; the truth of nature was unfolding in a way I had never imagined before.

Close to the backyard was a mountain slope with lush vegetation. The place was filled with a sense of abundance. The denseness, versatility, and uniqueness of each tree absorbed my attention.

Roshi had been enjoying this great landscape all by himself. I decided to tell him about my new awareness and completely forgot I had intended to go to the toilet.

I rushed back to his room and shouted, "Roshi, I had a breakthrough." I told him I knew exactly what wabi and sabi, elegant simplicity and tranquility, stood for. "Wabi and sabi are everywhere in ordinary things, but without the practice of zazen, I don't think I could ever have seen this!"

I laughed with delight.

In response, Roshi quietly said, "Life remains illusory and empty for people who rush to fill their time with activities. They take up hobbies and pastimes; otherwise they are bored and restless. The truth is that living in the present is the most fulfilling experience. There are many ways to express that sense of complete fulfillment. Wabi and sabi may be some of them. They basically point out that whatever and whoever you encounter right here and right now is pregnant with meaning. With nothing lacking and nothing excessive, it is just right and in its proper place. You do not have to make it happen. You do not have to look for it somewhere else. You do not have to get rid of anything. If your mind is non-attached and free-flowing, you can experience the fullness of each moment 'as it is'.

People might say it is too warm today to even talk about tasting the elegant simplicity of life, but this heat is itself elegant simplicity. Can you see what I mean?"

I interpreted Roshi's meaning to be that a high temperature is just that; experience it without thoughts and the mind is at peace. If we can simply live the circumstances of life as they are, that itself is absolute reality.

Later, I was sweeping the garden. I thought it would look beautiful if I left sweeping marks on the white sand in front of the main temple. I must have been walking from one end of the garden to the other and repeating this sweeping rather casually.

Suddenly I heard Roshi's angry voice. "You are slack! You are not mindful of your steps!"

Without a pause I responded, "I am focusing on just sweeping."

"How dare you say that? Don't you see you are lazy? Just because zazen is easier for you does not mean you can be complacent. If you are focused in this very moment, there is no room to relish the sweetness of your progress. When sweeping, concentrate thoroughly on sweeping and sweeping only. Do it with the greatest care; otherwise you will never ever find the illuminated path. You have to forget yourself completely and make yourself totally available to what you are doing right at this moment. If the practice appears easier, you have to double the intensity of your attention and sharpen your focus on the present."

I realized I had misunderstood the whole process of Zen practice. In the beginning, it was difficult and painful; I had no idea how to concentrate my mind on each breath. After I had figured it out, it was not so hard and I could see my own progress. So I assumed that the practice would turn out to be an increasingly easier experience. But it was not that simple. With only a glimpse of what is real, I had led myself to believe now my mind was liberated and had touched the Original Self. That itself was already a self-centered delusion. 'Peace of mind in being the present' was taken over by the thought of 'I now have peace of mind.' As a consequence, this thought had hindered my practice; I had grown slack about giving total attention to the immediate work right in front of me. The truth was that my mind had not freed itself from deluded thoughts at all.

Roshi then said, "The practice of Zen is always focused on 'living fully in the moment.' Regardless of whether you are a beginner or experienced, it requires persistent training to bring your mind back to this moment. In the beginning, you struggle to abandon your thoughts and return to what is happening now. With practice, the mind acquires the strength to let thoughts come and go without distracting your concentration. You gain profound equanimity. With further practice, you can catch the exact moment when the thought appears and disappears. Then you experience with certainty, 'Aha! This is the very moment!'"

He continued: "This original state of mind can be likened to the mind of a newborn. It is the stage of development before any formation of self-consciousness, stereotypes, or value judgments. This is the state of mind enabling shikan, or 'single-minded concentration in the present moment.' This is where the fully- fledged practice of Zen starts. Once you get to this stage, you will require less effort in aligning your mind. But you must not slacken your effort. Shikan must be practiced non-stop so you have direct experiences of shikan not just in zazen but in everything you do. This practice of complete mindfulness is an ongoing purification process, stripping off fantasies, prejudices, opinions, and judgments. This is extremely difficult because the source of what gives rise to these thoughts is still active in your mind. It is bound to be caught up by distracting thoughts unless you make a conscious and constant effort to bring your mind back into the present. Once you own the experience of realization, it stands in your way, separating you from your Original Self. Your very thought of having had an enlightenment experience blocks you from being free-flowing. Instead of holding onto it, you must leave this thought behind and continue rigorous practice so you are freshly born and reborn into the present. Only through persistent practice can your enlightenment become a solid and authentic experience. Therefore you need to step up your practice, especially after you have had a glimpse of your Original Self. Zen practice after enlightenment is all the more important because you are in a continual process of renewal; the past experience of shikan must be continually broken through, dropped, and replaced with the immediate experience of shikan. And when you even forget you are striving to be mindful and instead, just purely experience, everything you engage in becomes a manifestation of the Original Self. This is called 'great enlightenment' where every moment represents the eternal present, transcending life and death. It is an identical experience to the ultimate and supreme enlightenment the Buddha attained. In other words, his or her enlightenment experience is the same as the Buddha's. Those who reach this stage are called awakened ones. Students of Zen must not relax and indulge themselves in the world of elegant simplicity. They need to consciously make their life simple so they can keep up the momentum for their single-minded commitment to pursue the path. Otherwise, the bliss and exhilaration that unfolds with the practice of zazen will be dazzling and may carry you away from the original intent of practice. That is why having a Zen master as a guide is critical - students are encouraged to move on without getting caught up with their initial enlightenment experience."

Thanks to Roshi's words, by the time I had finished sweeping the garden, my euphoria was gone and my mind calm.

After a while, Mr. Waki, my colleague from high school, came to visit me. I could not figure out whether he came to give me support or to check out my progress. Being anxious to know more about Zen, he bombarded me with questions. The only thing I could tell him was that Zen is not fully describable or intellectually understandable to anyone without the actual practice of zazen. The only way to Zen is to practice for oneself.

Like me, only a few weeks before, Mr. Waki rushed to conceptualize Zen while not having the slightest idea of what he wanted to understand. He might ask me detailed questions on the internal changes that come with the practice, but no matter how I responded, they would be mere words to him; and words would be dangerous at this stage as they may prevent him from having any real experience of zazen.

It was amazing how I could read Mr. Waki's state of mind so clearly; it was different from guessing or speculating; I could see through it as if it was my own mind.

I raised this with Roshi and he said, "It is nothing special. When you grow more self-aware, you acknowledge you actually have every human attribute in yourself and therefore are more capable of relating to what is going on in the mind of others. So, if you want to understand others, it is essential that first you know who you really are."

Roshi is always to the point. What Roshi said in my first sesshin serves to this day as a powerful insight in my everyday interaction with my students. With Mr. Waki, all I could do was sincerely wish that he practice zazen, and I am pleased to note that he actually did start practicing zazen later on.

If we can gain more understanding of ourselves and others through practice, then what about Roshi, who has been practicing most of his life? Roshi must have penetrating insight into whatever or whoever forms a relationship with him. However, he openly admits that he is still confronted by one unresolved issue. I believe his honesty about this is a manifestation of his dedication to the teachings of the Buddha and perhaps a reflection of self-confidence. What if he resolves this last unresolved issue? Somehow it is both awesome and delightful to think about it.

That night I was fascinated by the tactile sensation of everything I touched; I roamed around, touching the sliding paper door, the tatami mat, a wooden pillar. Each object had profound presence; each had a uniquely different touch, yet they were all one and the same to me. It sounds illogical, but this is the only way I can describe the reality of the experience, a reality beyond reason.

Around 2:00 or 3:00 a.m., I could no longer stay still in the temple, and roamed through the town of Tadanoumi. Not a soul was on the streets but I did not feel lonely. With no boundary between myself and everything else, the space I was in was infinitely nourishing and inviting. The whole town loomed like an exquisite artificial flower, beautiful and surreal.

I was wide awake; my mind was absolutely clear and my body free from fatigue. For next few days, I never felt sleepy. After returning to the temple, I continued zazen till dawn. As the sky was turning lighter, I swept the sand garden. Dark lines made by the broom on the sand appeared distinctive and alive against the white background. The lines were dramatic; yet there was no heightened emotion and I was totally with what I saw and absolutely calm.

Fifth Day

Thus, on the fifth morning in the temple, I started sweeping the garden. Once the sun was out, it was steaming hot. After finishing the garden, I cleaned up the zendo and started zazen right away. Thoughts still kept coming up at random but my mind was hardly distracted by them. Because I did not react to them, they faded. My mind still carried its old habit of diffusing attention with constant chatter. The old roots were still alive underground; unless they withered, the mind would not be truly liberated. But if I left them alone and did not attend to them, they would eventually wither. It was different from passively waiting; when time matures, I know withering will be the natural course of events.

In the afternoon, an acquaintance of Roshi came to visit the temple. I joined them in Roshi's study. He was an inquisitive fellow and kept asking me questions. "What do you do for work? Oh, you teach in public high-school. So you are a public servant. Aren't you lucky you have no fear about going bankrupt? How much do you get paid? What about bonus payments? How many people in your family? What about your wife? You mean she is also a public servant? Two incomes must add up to a huge sum. I bet you earn so much that you don't know what to spend it on. Does zazen help you to make more money?" So it went on.

In the beginning, his voice was just meaningless sound passing through me. Gradually mere sound transformed into the voice of a person, and his words started to have meaning and arouse emotion.

Soon I was carefully choosing my words to respond to his questions. I asked myself, 'What's the point of asking all these questions? He has no manners. Isn't he a bore?'

The moment these thoughts came in, the equanimity of my mind was gone; it started whirling again.

How could I be disrupted so easily?

I had only spent a little time talking about this trivial stuff. I knew I would completely lose the tranquility of my mind if I stayed any longer. But I was not sure if it would be polite to excuse myself.

Then Roshi, sensing my embarrassment, said, "Mr. Jyuraku, you had better go. It doesn't do you any good being here."

Later Roshi said, "The serious path seeker must deliberately choose the right relationships so he or she can get to the path. You need to look for relationships that support you and benefit you in the process. At the same time, you have to be firm and brave in avoiding obstructive relationships. By relationship I mean both relationships to people and things."

He continued, "When you don't want to be seen as impolite, you do things just to keep up appearances. Meanwhile, your sense of being in the present quickly slips away, and you lose sight of the path. It is totally acceptable for students who are in the middle of sesshin to divorce themselves from what is considered socially appropriate behavior."

I did not need to worry whether excusing myself in the middle of a conversation would be impolite. The path seeker must focus only on the path and nothing else. If I know that the relationship is disruptive to my practice, I need to leave it immediately rather than waste my energy worrying what others might think of me. This would be an important reminder when I went back to my daily routine.

Soon I started to do zazen again but I had lost my tranquility. I tried to settle down but without success.

I thought trying in vain was a waste of time and went to Roshi for advice. He said, "Lie down and relax every part of your body. Be gentle with yourself. Stay still and keep staring at the ceiling."

For the next hour or two, I did exactly as he said; I focused on the ceiling while breathing slowly. After a while, it appeared as if the ceiling was breathing. There was no more self; no trace of disrupted mind; only the reality of being here as it was.

"Roshi! I've got it!"

I was so pleased I had to let him know immediately, even though he was in the middle of taking a bath.

The way these seven days of intense Zen practice was structured was very useful for me. Roshi was available whenever I needed his guidance. Each time he inspired me and encouraged me by sharing the profound wisdom of the Buddha which is hidden within all of us.

Roshi said, "You lost the equanimity of mind. But that is already a thing of the past. If you are wholly in the present, the past has no room to come in. You need to let the past go. The capacity to let go gives you the capacity to live moment by moment in fullness."

Roshi's advice to just lie down, breathe slowly and stare at the ceiling was very effective in ridding myself of restlessness and returning to a point with no accompanying thoughts.

Sixth Day

Next day I wanted to see Mr. Kozumi, so I got permission from Roshi to call on him. However, the moment I saw him, I felt the whole purpose of my visit was attained and I wanted to leave. Within only a few minutes of chat, the disquieting thought of losing my groundedness took over.

I said to him, "I must go! I am losing the sense of being in harmony with the present. It's slipping out of me. I am restless again." And with that, I dashed back to do zazen in the zendo.

If my mind started spinning as soon as I left the zendo, what was I going to do when I went back to normal life? That was an awesome challenge. That night I stayed up and did zazen the whole night.

Both Mr. Kozumi and Mr. Nagaoka, who had started to practice zazen right after Mr. Kozumi, warned me that the sense of total mindfulness in the present may slip out of my mind within a matter of thirty minutes after leaving the temple. I already knew what that was like even while I was in the temple. So I spent the rest of my time training my mind to stay focused on the moment. Especially when I walked on the street, I tried to concentrate on just seeing or just hearing, without being distracted by aural and visual stimuli. In order to avoid my mind becoming prey to external stimuli, I worked on myself to abandon thoughts the instant they emerged. This gave me some confidence in controlling my mind.

Seventh Day

At last the day had arrived, and I was to leave the temple.

"Mr. Jyuraku, where you are standing now is only the gateway to the path of Zen. Don't ever think you have found a special passport to cruise along the path. You have just only found the main path to Zen practice. Unless you have total dedication and thorough commitment to keep practicing, you will lose all and return to restlessness and confusion. I say this, because 'this moment' is nothing but this immediate moment. Likewise, your state of mind in the moment is only valid in the moment. With the passage of time, the state of mind keeps changing. Being wholly present means accepting the reality that nothing stays the same; everything is impermanent and we cannot be attached to certain states of mind. That is exactly why being fully present is so liberating. This very moment is an ever-purifying and renewing moment; its only permanent truth is impermanence. You must be determined to continue to practice and walk along the path of Zen. Wherever you go or whatever you do, you are yourself, experiencing what is in that moment. So, be totally mindful, moment by moment. As dedicated practice builds, eventually your mind will experience great enlightenment."

These were his last words before I left. He had made himself totally available for one-on-one guidance, and moreover, I had been privileged to use Kaizoji for my practice.

The seven-day sesshin was like standing at the junction of heaven and hell. Thanks to Roshi and his wife, I could leave this place feeling totally invigorated. Seeing Roshi so pleased with my progress made me feel even more grateful to him.

Late in the afternoon, my wife arrived with our two children to pick me up.

"Dad, your face looks refreshed," said my children.

We were delighted to see each other.

After paying sincere tributes to Roshi, we left the temple. As soon as I said farewell, I made a conscious effort not to lose the sense of being in the moment in the new environment. As I looked through the car window, everything - trees, ocean, houses – was sparkling; it was as though I saw this familiar landscape for the first time.

I was also aware of the inquisitive eyes of my family but I knew I could not share the experience of 'just being' with them. They were remote from what I had been through. That did not mean I felt lonely; on the contrary, I was more aware of their clear presence and preciousness.

I had been away for only a week. While nothing had changed at home, it was all new to me. In our family, we tease each other and laugh at light jokes. But I did not feel like doing this anymore. Obviously a gap had opened up between my family and me. I knew it and they knew it. I was so anxious about losing my equanimity. More than ever now I was aware of how much they meant to me, but if I expressed this, would I align myself with their scattered minds? Would I lose the groundedness of just being in the moment? Would my mind start spinning and spreading thin? Of course, after a while, even though I worked hard to remain in focus, my mind was being slowly eroded by waves of emotion.

First Day after Sesshin

Next morning I woke up early. This was my time of solitude in the family. I started zazen immediately. It was exciting to discover I could still experience the sense of being totally alive in the moment. It did not wither or fade. I called up Roshi to report this pleasing outcome.

Before my call, Roshi had assumed that I had completely lost it. So, as soon as he picked up the phone, he said, "Tell me your impression of hell!"

"No way, Roshi!"

He was delighted to know how I had gone with my practice that morning.

* * * * * * * * * * *

Following my example, Mr. Waki also joined an intense zazen sesshin. Like myself, he was able to experience being in the absolute moment of now through his practice. That was encouraging for me; now I had a colleague with whom I could share a common interest.

The summer holiday was over, and school started. While commuting, I was stunned by the beauty of landscapes which I had never noticed before. There was a sense of bliss. Moreover, I realized driving was much easier; this, by the way, was echoed by other Zen students as well. I had not anticipated Zen practice could relax the mind and improve one's driving. Previously I must have been wasting energy by being too tense. I suppose stillness of mind facilitates seeing the whole picture and what needs to be done with minimum effort.

Zen practice had an immense impact on my professional life as well. In my first class after the holiday, as I stood in front of the class, I felt a close affinity with each student. I could, without any effort, embrace who they were as they were in their uniqueness. My underlying fear and anxiety of being inadequate had dissipated. It was like a mirror which had been cleaned; I could see the emotional and mental state of each student with much greater clarity. This led me to be more relaxed and self-confident and enabled me to talk to students without reservation. The distance that used to set me apart from my students had narrowed. As a result, they started to drop in for guidance or counseling, which I consider a great privilege. I know all these changes stem from the power of being in the moment.

I still get distracted easily, due to inadequate inner strength; this happens especially when mixing with large numbers of people; I start to judge, analyze, and project rather than be free from thoughts.

In my desperate attempt to protect 'just being,' I sometimes avoid chatting with my colleagues in the teachers' room. I turn away from them and practice deep slow breathing. I must appear inaccessible at times.

When moving between the teachers' room and the classroom, I am absolutely serious about completely being 'just that step.' One day, I was so absorbed in each step that I did not realize my students were walking with me, keeping time with the pace of my steps, and saying "one, two, and one, two." To date, they still do this for me while I practice concentrating on each step.

During breaks, I do zazen in the school warehouse. Sometimes, if Mr. Waki is sitting there ahead of me, I go to another warehouse so I won't disturb his practice. Seeing him sitting with such persistence is silent but strong encouragement to keep up with my own practice. I am glad to have a like-minded colleague around me. At other times, I do zazen on top of my desk in the teachers' room.

Others must think I am mad.

Letting go of disturbing thoughts still feels excruciating at times. I even thought I might develop an ulcer. Roshi's advice was, "Maximize your stress. Maximum concentration is derived from maximum stress. Think that this is the only chance you will get in life to return to this very moment. Then, even if you lose yourself in thoughts, you can come back to the moment quickly and restore clarity and peace of mind."

He was again right to the point.

As I look back over the two years since I first started zazen, the changes are clearly enormous. Now, I hardly ever get disrupted by whom I meet or where I am. My mind can rest in stillness and equanimity. My concentration has improved by leaps and bounds. It has become my routine to visit Roshi. Even when I feel restless and out of focus, I settle down by just visiting him. He is generous with his time and energy, sharing the wisdom of Buddhahood. Thanks to him, I am more familiar with the concepts and ideas embodied in Buddhism. What is most pleasing is that in the last two years more than ten dedicated students have knocked at the gate of the temple, asking for permission to do intense zazen practice.

It is only a matter of making a week available for practice. Anyone can do it. The hard part is to continue to practice when we re-enter normal life.

If the practice had ended for me after one week in the zendo, it might have been nothing more than one of those unusual experiences in life that fades over time. Unless we constantly renew our awareness of the importance of caring for our spirit and keep up with our practice, we will not cultivate inner strength.

What are the absolute requisites for Zen practice?

The most important driving force for us students is the yearning to search for the path and the determination to live moment by moment with utmost mindfulness. It is also imperative to just listen to what Roshi is pointing out to us and practice in good faith. Lastly, we need to find the right teacher who can guide us by the most direct route to the path; we need a guide so we can personally experience being on the path. This, I think, is the hardest of all the requisites. However, provided that they are met, I can say with every confidence that the path to liberation of mind is open to all of us.

POSTSCRIPT

Every so often Roshi's students get together; we enjoy sharing our experiences, ranging from how each of us manages to set time aside for Zazen, to what unfolds as we progress in our practice.

One day, we all agreed that listening to each other's experience was extremely useful and stimulating for our own practice. With this is mind, we decided to write our personal stories of our Zen experience.

Having listened to Roshi's sermons many times, I was confident that I could quote him and convey the real essence of what he intended to say with a fair degree of accuracy. So Roshi only skimmed through my notes before they were sent to the printing house. Actually these are only excerpts of countless sermons; I deliberately kept them brief because eloquence does not mean a thing if we do not practice zazen.

Before I finish, I would like to quote a few more lines from Roshi's sermons that have made a strong impression on me.

"All you need to do is to be totally in the present. There is nothing else. If you believe this and commit yourself to 'just being,' that is all you need to know. The core of practice is 'just sitting.' Sermons are better if kept brief. The reason why I talk it through is because most people cannot trust that doing zazen or just sitting is the essence of practice. So I use words as a vehicle to open them up and instill faith in their practice."

"Honoring the path of Zen means revering those path seekers and explorers who have opened the path before us. Only those who take the path seriously for themselves can embrace the full meaning of their teachings."

I should also add a supplementary comment to a quotation of Roshi's when he said, "Maximum concentration is derived from maximum stress." I am afraid I might have been too brief to convey the whole scope of what he meant by this statement. Zen students like us live in the hustle and bustle of everyday life; we get easily carried away by people around us. We only have a glimpse of becoming present, and that is not powerful enough to pull our minds back from thinking this and that. Some thoughts linger on; we are left in anguish because we want to get rid of them but they persist. Roshi's comment dealt with a practical way to deal with such a situation. That is, when we are haunted by guilt, anger, grief, anxiety, bitterness, depression, attachments to illusion, and any churning thinking, we ought to stand on the cutting edge, and maximize the stress so we have no choice but to be in the moment and come back to the path. Then we regain clarity of mind.

At first it puzzled me why people with problems started to come to me for help after I started zazen, but when I am totally committed to my practice, I can offer them clear-cut and candid advice.

However, when I am stuck and out of touch with myself, I muddle and mumble in hesitation. This is because when I lose the clarity of my own mind, I am unable to see the mind of other people clearly. These experiences make me humble and, every time they happen, I renew my resolve to go deeper into my practice.

DISCOVERING MY DIAMOND LIFE

...

BY: AZUSA KAKENO

DISCOVERING
MY DIAMOND LIFE

• • •

Azusa Kakeno
President of an accounting
firm/ born in 1941

The flight from Taipei to Japan was quiet and without turbulence. My two week trip to Peru, Brazil, and Taiwan was coming to an end.

I met many wonderful people. Particularly I loved the enthusiasm of the Peruvians. I remembered Peruvian President Fujimori spraying water from a huge hose over a crowd of villagers during an inauguration ceremony, celebrating the turning on of the first tap at the summit of Los Andes. Joy and gratitude shone on the people's faces as they enjoyed the feeling of fresh water drenching their bodies. At last they had access to tap water. Their cries of joy echoed through the mountains of Los Andes and into the clearest blue sky, a magical moment of beauty, interweaving nature, human beings, and all that is sacred. There were radiant faces and tears of gratitude for this time of grace. Just looking at those faces was so healing and nourishing.

Didn't we once have the same sparkling eyes and big smiles as those villagers in Peru?

But when, exactly? The first time I saw that same big smile ... seemed many years ago...

*   *   *

Oh! It just kicked," the woman said..

"Must be a healthy baby." The man said. "I hope it is a girl."

She replied "As long as it's a healthy baby, I am happy with either. But I have a feeling 'it' is a 'she'"

"Well, you may be right," the man said

I hear the voices in the distance, gentle comfortable voices, for which I somehow feel great nostalgia. Voices of a man and a woman. What are they talking about? They sound very happy. Please talk louder so I can hear you! No? My voice does not seem to reach them. Can't you hear me? Please, I am talking to you. Doesn't seem to work. But O.K.

Soon I will talk to them. How? I don't know how, but I know it's going to happen.

With warm, soft water surrounding me, I am light and floating. Though naked, I am not cold at all. It is so cozy here. I want to stay here forever.

My goodness! What a strange sensation!

The warm water around me is starting to move. My body is rolling. Something is about to happen. Forming a gentle swirl, the water is being sucked into a tunnel. The swirl is carrying my body down, slowly.

Where to?

No, I don't want to leave here. I want to stay here, floating forever. But I am being pulled down by an incredible power I cannot resist. The swirl is growing stronger. I had better let myself go with it.

"Waaahhh."

"Congratulations! It's a beautiful girl. She looks very well" the doctor said

The woman replied "Thank you."

People are welcoming my arrival into this world. Everyone around me is smiling with joy, that same big smile of the villagers in Los Andes.

Someone in a white dress holds me in her arms, wipes my body, and wraps me in a new cloth. She then puts me close to a woman who is lying down, looking exhausted, a woman with a kindly face, glowing with tears of joy.

"What a lovely, healthy baby! Thank you for coming to us, baby."

[I had heard her voice before. Oh! Yes, the couple who had been happily talking ... that woman's voice.]

"So glad to see you, baby. I am your mother."

[Mother? Now I know that woman was my mother.]

"Bravo! So it is born!"

[Oh! That man's voice ... I had also heard it before.]

"Darling, our baby is a 'she'!"

"Well done, sweetheart!"

"I knew it was a girl."

"You were absolutely right. I'm glad everything went so well."

[Both of my parents are extremely happy; everyone is delighted.
But I am still not used to this bright light; its stimulation is too strong
for me.]

"Congratulations! Well done!"

"Pardon? What did you say just now?"

"Eh?"

"I heard you say 'it's beautiful.'"

I awoke from a dream. I remembered I was on the flight back to Japan.
"No, nothing really. It's an old memory ..."

Mr Yazaki, who was sitting next to me, stopped marking the thick book
he was reading. "Azusa-san, I bet you've been enjoying your dream. You were
talking in your sleep. You'd better give me hush money so I don't tell anybody.
Ha! Ha! Ha!" he said with hearty laughter.

"Not again, Mr. Yazaki! I know what you're alluding to. By now, I've
learned to live with your jokes. Isn't it strange how I listen to whatever you
say? I guess it is because I feel you're like my father!"

Spontaneously I linked arms with him. The warmth coming through felt like a father's touch.

There was something mysterious about this trip. I had found myself seated next to Mr, Yazaki on every flight and bus trip. And, for some reason, he kept talking passionately about Inoue Kido Roshi, the Abbot of Shorinkutsu Seminary. Unlike those somebodies famous in name but not in substance whom we often come across and get disillusioned by, this Roshi sounded like a nobody, but with real substance. But why did he always talk about Roshi? The instant I asked myself this question, I was struck with an insight. 'Azusa, perhaps it's your own yearning to hear about Roshi that encourages Mr Yazaki to speak of him?' Of course. That was it!

"Mr. Yazaki!"

"Yes, Azusa-san. What's the matter with you? All of sudden you look so serious!"

"Please, let me meet with Inoue Roshi."

Amazingly quick to respond, Mr. Yazaki opened up his diary on the spot.

"Azusa-san, when are you available? You had better leave one week completely open."

"Eh? One whole week? The only time I can take time off would be between the year-end and the New Year holiday. I will check with my office when I return."

Once Mr. Yazaki got back to Japan, he would probably forget about my request because of his imminent trip to Australia. Mr. Yazaki is deeply committed to the education of future generations and is continually on the run, making visits all over the world. So I took his response with a grain of salt. I never expected that our conversation would find me dashing along the path towards enlightenment.

The rapture I had witnessed in the people of Peru belonged to a clear, unclouded spirit; it was a quality that the Japanese had long forgotten even existed. The enthusiastic reception that we received from first-generation Japanese entrepreneurs in Brazil was also very moving. And people we met in Taiwan, too. I felt I was being thrown into the huge, invisible vortex of a larger resonance.

"I know a new door is opening for me," I murmured to myself.

Already, our plane had started to make a big circle. Beneath us were the million sparkling lights of Tokyo, looking like the galaxy. The illuminations on the runway were getting closer, and the plane would soon land at Narita Airport.

First Day

I changed trains from the Shinkan-sen to the Kure line at Mihara station. There were hardly any passengers on this local train with only two cars. The train ran along the coastal edge close to the Seto Inland Sea, and the views from the train were just splendid.

Does the sparkling sea resemble a bright diamond? I mused, looking out the train window, or is it the diamond that reminds me of the sparkling sea? Is our fascination with its radiance because our spirit is inherently as bright as a diamond?

Initially, I couldn't appreciate the serenade of gentle waves and lights. I had just squeezed time out of a very busy year-end schedule. But so glorious was the scenery of the numerous islands and calm water that I was eventually captivated by its exquisite beauty, forgetting for a while the austerity of Zen practice that awaited me.

I had been holding some unresolved questions - I don't know for how long - that I knew could be taken care of only in the realm of my soul. Over recent years, I had a growing need to address them and, hopefully, let them go. Jumping into an institutionalized religion was not on my agenda. However, I wanted to be totally honest in addressing my needs. To me, making a sincere effort to reach for a deeper level was basically the same as religious practice. Any indoctrination or blind acceptance of ideas is ephemeral, for it contains the inherent risk of collapse. When ideas are imposed by someone else, they lack the authenticity of ideas which rise from within. What I wanted was to learn a truly workable process that could help me delve into the essence of my being, into my authentic self. So the karmic relationship that later unfolded between Roshi and me was by no means accidental. It was a golden thread I had consciously drawn in to be interwoven into my journey.

At noon I arrived at Tadanoumi station. Roshi and his disciple, Mr. Yusetsu, kindly met me at the station to take me to Shourinkutsu Seminary. Freed from my super-tight work schedule, I was grateful for this opportunity; it felt like attending the sort of workshop I had never attended before. There was neither fear nor anxiety; during their warm welcome, the only thing in my head was that I was going to do my best to honor this opportunity.

My professions are tax accounting and management consulting. Our busiest season is from December to the end of March, yet, here I was about to start my sesshin from the twenty-second to the twenty-ninth of December. The time must surely have been ripe for my encounter with Roshi.

The reason I could take this break without any worry were my great employees, whom I could trust entirely; I felt extremely fortunate and appreciative of them. My employees are my treasures. I sincerely wish to share a life of integrity and happiness with them. My employees are my family through work. As we have shared the longest span of our lives together, we have naturally become life partners.

I can remember as if it were yesterday, studying for the national examination to become a licensed tax accountant, while raising my young children, then five and three, as a single mother. There could be no room for self-doubt; I just kept working at it and passed the exam. But not a single accounting office would give me an interview because I was a woman and, on top of that, I had young children who still needed a lot of care. The only choice left for me was to set up my own accounting firm. Thus, I was able to continue raising my two children, whom I had always regarded as my mentors. Inexperienced as I was, I had to make a leap and become an entrepreneur from the outset of my career.

Because I dared to take up a management role, I had to be doubly serious about my own growth. And I also had faith that, if I asked, there would be always an encounter with the right person at the right time.

So I was grateful for the series of events that led me to meet Roshi. As he led me to the Seminary, I raised my hands, palm-to-palm and, in silence, spoke to his back, "Roshi, I am looking forward to your compassionate guidance."

I was assigned a three-tatami room to the left of the Seminary entrance; the room had only one old desk, no curtain on the window, and a sliding paper door. My immediate response was, "Oh! It's freezing cold!" But soon I forgot about that as I changed into a kimono and hakama. These traditional costumes, although not practical and hardly worn these days, seemed to have a mind-calming effect.

After changing, I walked quietly to Roshi's interview room at the end of the corridor for his talk on the basics of Zen practice.

He said, "You must detach yourself from your small self to reach your own depths. Being thoroughly absorbed in what you are doing right this moment is the way to detachment. You become one indivisible whole with whatever you are engaged in. You become simple, perhaps a complete fool, wiping away all your intellectualizing processes, your own judgments and opinions. Be just as you are and simply do it. But I warn you, it isn't easy to relinquish your deeply entrenched habits. Any slackness will pull you back to old patterning. So you need to be absolutely serious about bringing your mind into focus."

Most of what Roshi was saying was commonsense and easy to follow. But was it possible to stop intellectualizing activity and make no judgments at all? Wouldn't it disrupt our everyday lives, if we did that? Naturally, if we did slow down our intellectualizing activity, we would carry less of a mental burden. But mental burdens can be alleviated by distractions, while the causes of mental burden remain unresolved. I wondered how Zen would address my question.

Roshi went on, "The first and most important key to Zen practice is where you focus your mind, the right orientation to your practice. Even with the slightest deviation, you will not get to your final destination. The second key is sincere application. Without each step taken, there is no progress whatsoever. The last key is continuity of application. Let me ask you, who ensures this continuity?"

The first two keys were what we entrepreneurs talk about all the time in achieving a business target. But the last key made me flustered. Of course, I had anticipated that Roshi was going to challenge me with some confronting questions. They came, however, too soon; this question was too difficult, and my own reasoning was inadequate.

"Isn't it myself?" I responded with some vagueness. What was the matter with me? Usually I would be much more definitive.

"Who confuses yourself?"

"I think it is myself."

"Then, who saves yourself?"

"I think it is also myself."

"Right! Then when is the time for your salvation or confusion?"

I had never heard any theory in the past that addressed states of mind through the perspective of time. It was mind-boggling and quite persuasive but I felt I needed an entirely new circuit in my brain to integrate it.

"Everything begins with oneself and ends with oneself. The mind is free and flexible and goes through ceaseless transformations of bringing yourself into being and passing away, from one moment to next. The mind is fully available to everything and attached to nothing. It is impermanent and unfixed in nature. When you realize that is the essence of your mind, there is nothing that binds you. This is enlightenment ... you move beyond your small self."

I had a gut feeling about the authenticity of his remarks and made up my mind on the spot to surrender to his guidance.

Roshi continued, "The question is how to attain enlightenment? This is where the battle starts. So I want you to listen carefully. You will need to break away from the control of your intellectualizing process that sees everything as separate. To do this, you will need first to draw a clear boundary between the absolute reality of the present moment and the limited reality of your conceptualizing mind. Zen calls for you to be completely absorbed in the moment. Or to put it another way, complete absorption is both the goal and fruit of Zen practice; and Zen teaches you a method to get to that state of intense concentration. When you are completely absorbed, you are merged into a single unity with absolute reality at any given time. When you are merged into a single unity, you are so simplified that you become identical with the things around you and you forget about yourself altogether. When you forget about yourself, you awaken to the truth of the universe, right at that instant. When you awaken, you realize your freedom, from suffering and delusion through seeing each thing, just 'as it is'. You become capable of drawing a boundary between the past and present, and by so doing, you can remove the barrier that separates you from the rest. That is all there is about attaining oneness. With enlightenment, you have a heightened awareness of this essential reality. Rather than endlessly letting your mind churn with random thoughts, just absorb yourself in a single breath. Keep up your intense concentration with every single breath and you will be fine. Focus your mind. This is a life and death matter. That is all I need to tell you now."

I was afraid I could not fully understand Roshi's statement that drawing a boundary between the past and present is basically the same thing as removing the barrier that separates me from the rest.

'That's normal,' I said to myself; I would not be able to appreciate everything from Day One. Better to hold fast to a single breath, as he said.

We were served a bowl of hot noodles for lunch. I was happy to feel the steam from the boiling pot, giving off precious heat. The five of us ate intently; other than the noise of blowing and supping hot soup and noodles, an enigmatic silence prevailed, with no conversation. It was like a wake. But the mystery was quickly solved.

After lunch, a just few steps along the corridor, Roshi shouted, "Give your whole attention to each step!"

As I had known from hearsay, he was very strict, and not just strict. His deep, strong voice was scary. I did not know when or how my attention had slipped as I walked, but I knew I was not fully alert. I renewed my determination to sustain my concentration.

I sat from 1 p.m. to 6 p.m. in the zendo. Five hours of zazen went by very quickly. But paying attention to each single breath was far more difficult than I had thought; I had been so used to breathing without any awareness. 'It isn't impossible. I just have to keep trying,' I said to myself.

After supper, from 7:30 to 9 p.m, I went into the zendo to sit. The temperature went down further at night; it was biting cold.

When I returned to my room at 9:30 p.m., I was too cold to undress, and slipped into my futon in my kimono. Please excuse my negligence.

Second Day

I got up at 4:30 a.m. and started zazen in the zendo half an hour later.

The hard, piercing throb of the percussive wooden board penetrated my entire nervous system; I felt as if each throb was building up a certain momentum in my heart and body, and soon I might disintegrate. With exquisite timing, the thumping was followed by the temple bell from the bottom of the Seminary and, though freezing cold, I became enfolded in the pleasant tension of a Zen temple, with no option but to strive to do my best. Even with the gloves Roshi had lent me, my hands were numb. There was no way to make myself warmer. I regretted that I had not given serious thought to the coldness of the Zen temple and prepared myself for it with adequate clothing.

At 6 a.m. we started morning practice in the main hall of the temple. I tried to follow and chant the sutras as well as I could. At 7 a.m. we ate breakfast consisting of steamed rice, toasted nori, pickles, nattoh, kelp cooked in soy, and himono (cured fish). I was relishing my breakfast when Roshi's stern words suddenly startled me.

"Ms. Kakeno, you need to be truly focused on each bite, rather than just eating casually. That is the only truth you need to know right this instant. If you slacken your attention from 'just eating,' you are missing an opportunity for knowing the truth."

A new insight struck me suddenly. Roshi's earlier comment on my walking was pointing out exactly the same thing. 'Settle into the absolute reality of this very moment. Do not digress from the purity of the experience,' was his point. In spite of my resolve to apply myself to my practice, the reality was that it was incredibly hard to sustain such scrupulous focus on the moment. I was used to being scattered. Up until 8:30 a.m. I cleaned up the zendo, so absorbed that after I finished, I had no impression of what I had done. It was refreshing to have nothing to dwell on.

I sat for four hours in the morning and five hours in the afternoon in the zendo. Although I could not concentrate at times because of my aching legs, the zazen posture itself was not a major effort. I was used to sitting. The only annoyance was a persistent mantra I had been taught ages ago; this mantra kept coming back, no matter how much I tried to cut it off. I tried to be mindful of each breath, to be in tune with my breath, and to merge into my breath. Still, my breathing was not steady, sometimes fast, other times slow, and at other times completely taken over as thoughts sneaked in. How hard it was to be truly focused solely on the present, because my mind was not aligned with stillness. That was why I had come here to practice. If I could settle into profound stillness, my mind would not be the source of confusion any more. Anyway, I had no choice other than working on myself by myself.

'Focus on this instant. Direct your attention only to each single breath,' I kept reminding myself.

I tried to muster enough concentration to resist my old habit of drifting into random thoughts.

'That's it! That's brilliant!' The moment I praised myself I was already pulled into another labyrinth of thought. I found this repetitious challenge quite fascinating. Perhaps I was weird to be so fascinated by such a simple process.

After supper, Roshi said, "I expected you to reach the limits of your zazen today. Honestly, I was looking forward to seeing you slip back into confusion. But the truth is, you have moved beyond that stage. Already you are well on the way."

I told Roshi that I had had some glimmer of understanding in the past and described that moment, four years before, when I had felt my mind suddenly explode and with it, everything - judgments, frustration, resentments - spin away into eternity and dissolve forever. An inexplicable experience!

"I was stuck at an intersection in a heavy traffic jam in downtown Osaka," I told Roshi. "It all happened unexpectedly, and I had no idea what it was about. Once the traffic signal changed, I had to keep on driving. I was too overwhelmed even to worry about it. Tears rolled down my cheeks. The revelation that streamed up from the unconscious was that everything - every sentient being - is a manifestation of love, and I have nothing to fear."

I explained to Roshi that at the time, I had been confronted with a serious problem. It had dissolved in an instant, transformed into an opportunity for 'love and appreciation'. What a phenomenal blessing! I told Roshi that I had no teacher at that time, but that I believed one day I would meet the right teacher and the implication of that experience would be brought to my full awareness. That right teacher was Inoue Roshi, now sitting before me.

"Ms. Kakeno, just pursue your breath single-mindedly," said Roshi finally.

I did not realize we had continued our dialogue for well over two hours; the time went so fast.

That night as I slipped into the futon, I repeated the words I had pledged to Roshi earlier that evening - "I am determined to practise with my highest commitment." I whispered this to myself again and again. While whispering, my focus held fast onto every breath.

Third Day

I woke up at 4:30 a.m. and went to the zendo at 5 a.m. This morning it was exceptionally cold, most likely well below zero degrees Celsius. I was 'just' listening quietly - to the sound of the percussive wooden board. Why was my response so different from yesterday? There was profound stillness through the zendo, except that I was still struggling with my thoughts and breathe.

After breakfast, I went back to the zendo and sat from 8 a.m. to noon. I decided to do something about my aching legs. Rather than persevere with the pain, why not use three mats and a round cushion, as though sitting on a chair? Roshi's flexibility about sitting positions was a saving grace. Now my zazen was easier physically and allowed me to sustain a more distinctive focus on each breath.

Lunch was a bowl of steamed rice and stew.

"Ms. Kakeno, what is the taste?" asked Roshi abruptly.

"It is very tasty."

"No, that's not what I am asking. What is the taste?"

"It is the taste of stew and steamed rice."

"What is the taste?"

"..."

"Stop messing around with your thoughts. What is the taste?"
"It is the taste of this moment."

My mind had gone completely blank and I could no longer eat anything.

"Can't you just be and simply eat it?" Roshi shouted at me and left the room.

"..."

Vexed, I found no words to say. He was relentless. I had tried to make sense of his question but he would not accept my response.

Taste was taste. If asked what was the taste right this moment, the only response ought to be 'just eating'. Away with my old habits! No more conceptualizing! I should have just eaten single-mindedly - just eating, not thinking, just eating, not intellectualizing. By the time I realized the appropriate response to his question, it was too late. Meanwhile, I had been swayed by ceaseless thoughts, attempting to find the right answer. I went back to the zendo.

At 3 p.m. the beating of wooden clappers called us to the dining room again. I gave my undivided attention to each step so I could remain intimate with the state of zazen. Concentration and diligence seemed to be the foundation of Zen practice.

It was encouraging to notice my progress. Compared with the first day, when I had found setting my mind on each step insurmountably difficult, my mind was now completely in focus with each step as I followed Roshi's instruction and kept up my practice.

Other than calmness and peace, there wasn't anything extraordinary. I had finally settled, feeling deeply in tune and at home. I did not know when I had entered this realm. It was miraculous.

What? Goodies! A cake and a pot of tea on the table.

Then, another miraculous moment unfolded. The moment I saw the cake, everything - all my personal feelings and ideas - suddenly dissolved and disappeared completely, an experience of emptiness. Roshi would scold me for my arrogance if I said it was an enlightenment experience, but the experience was really clear and powerful. No longer there was any vestige of emotion or thoughts. Just myself, my pure essence. Similarly, everything I saw was its pure essence. As my hand picked up the cup of tea, and brought a piece of cake into my mouth, it was as if my hands had absolute autonomy. There was no 'I' who was moving my hands or relishing the cake, only the luminosity of being fully present in each moment.

This experience brought a complete renewal of my senses; the familiar scene was startlingly fresh. I truly tasted cake for the first time in my life. Yes, now at last I could 'just breath' as well.

Unleashed from thoughts and feelings, there was nothing to block me from attaining oneness with breathing. It was a reassuring, calming, and somewhat inspiring revelation.

I went back to the zendo immediately after tea. Breathing was incredibly easy. I could cut off myself from any thoughts, let them go, and return to breathing. Fantastic! Zazen had turned into a most fulfilling process.

By 6 p.m., with darkness falling, the zendo was getting freezing cold.

Something clicked as I sensed the chilliness. With no exaggeration, it was my second experience of realization. Needless to say, I still had a long way to go before attaining the Great Enlightenment of the Buddha or the masters of old. But to me, this was crossing into a new realm. 'I am alive. Therefore, I am breathing' is commonsense knowledge. While it is a scientific and valid piece of knowledge, that knowing only comes from the level of consciousness that interprets and conceptualizes reality.

The new realm that had opened up for me in this instant was where I was just breathing, and where each breath was dynamic and flowing. Unhindered by thoughts, the realm of 'just that' was fully alive in its own right.

To express 'the glory of aliveness', we usually tap into our feelings and emotion and we resort to our emotional capacity to feel its breadth and depth. However, 'the glory of aliveness' that filled me then was both the solid sense of being and the transparency of being just as I am, beyond layers of emotion, and even beyond any feeling of glory. I'd better not be euphoric. It would not be an authentic experience until Roshi recognized it.

So I reported to Roshi. As I sat in front of him and talked, my gratitude streamed through me, and I wept with joy.

"Where you have reached is the result of hard practice. But you have only begun to have a clearer awareness of the moment. Be attentive to each moment. The level of concentration you have attained is still tenuous and could get easily disrupted, if you relax. You cannot afford to be pleased with your progress; you are only at the entry point of real practice," said Roshi with absolute severity.

Beneath Roshi's strict words were his unspoken compassion and wisdom pointing to the much larger life which had quietly trickled into my heart. My tears dropped on his black wooden table as I felt embraced by the largeness of his being.

"It's Christmas Eve tonight. Let's have a joint celebration of both your effort and Christmas Eve, so the celebration can further motivate you to be attentive," suggested Roshi.

It was my mid-sesshin treat.

It seemed Roshi already knew in advance exactly what was going to happen with my practice. In recognition of my effort, I had the privilege of being the first person to take a bath that evening. As it was my first bath this sesshin, it was especially pleasurable. The sound of hot water as I poured it over my body, the sensation of gently immersing my body into the warm bath - each single event was startlingly vivid.

'I am truly alive!'

Enjoying a warm bath in total tranquility heightened that sense of aliveness. A moment of deep happiness.

I was aware that Mr Yusetsu, Roshi's disciple, had prepared this bath for me by burning wood outside the building in the cold. I was appreciative of his quiet support for my practice. Mr. Yusetsu, a graduate from the prestigious Kyoto University, had been well on his career path as a laser beam specialist but, knowing the career would not ultimately fulfill his aspirations, he had quit and begun practicing zazen in search of his life path. One day he came across the first edition of Roshi's book, Zazen: The Way to Awakening. With this book as a trigger, he vowed to practice Zen under Roshi's guidance and was ordained to the priesthood. His singular zeal was an inspiration to me.

I went back to the zendo after supper. The evening must have been the coldest that year. Indescribably cold. But zazen brought me to an ever deeper level of concentration. My practice was becoming an increasingly simple, pure, and satisfying experience.

Fourth Day

At 5 a.m. I went to the zendo.

While trying to settle my mind in zazen, Roshi came into the zendo and quietly put a blanket around me. Then he whispered, "You need to sustain your attention on your breath."

'Gracious! How does he know?' I was braced by his penetrating observation.

During the morning service, Roshi asked, "Ms. Kakeno, what is walking?"

In response, I simply walked.

At last, I had passed his test. It was so simple. But if I had muddled about with words, even something as natural as walking could turn into a source of confusion, ending up in 'the trap of our own imagining and reasoning', as Roshi described it. I could now discern the clear boundary between reality-as-it-is and theorized reality, the product of intellectual constructs. After removing theory, opinions, judgments and imaginings, the only thing left is reality-as-it-is.

Roshi said, "If we want to liberate ourselves from our old habit of displacing reality with theory and containing ourselves in a world of virtual image, we must direct full attention to each moment. For instance, when we see, we tend to become a captive of what we see. Why? It is because of our habitual patterning; a certain visual stimulation immediately triggers encoded knowledge and cognitive responses like a conditioned reflex, and that reflex often tends to be confrontational, separating the seer and the seen. That is the essential feature of the ego."

Roshi continued quietly, "But that particular piece of knowledge triggered by a certain visual stimulation is merely the product of the past. When we interpret present reality by dwelling on the past and extrapolating from the past, we live in delusion, in an imaginary world where reality is turned upside-down."

His last comment especially went like a bullet to my heart. "Strengthen your resolve to experience the truth of reality-as-it-is. You must never sidetrack your attention away from the moment. Concentrate unremittingly only on the moment, on every single breath. Do you understand?"

That was the most compelling sermon I had yet heard to make me focus on each decisive moment. Inspired by Roshi's encouragement, I threw myself into zazen. Insights came one after another. Zazen was becoming a supreme joy.

As there is a beginning, there is an ending. As there is an ending, there is a beginning.

Each moment is a start and at the same time, a completion. Delve into the depth of this truth. Grasp this original truth. With the eye, see myself, see my true self, see my heart and soul in this very instant. I am the wall and I am the sliding door. It sounds absurd. But how else can I describe the intimacy of merging with them as they come into sight. With each exhalation, I release, leave behind and break free from my ego. There, I see the truth. With each inhalation, I become one with the air I inhale as I let myself go. There, I see the truth. My ears have been given to hear the truth. If my ears fail to listen to the truth, nothing is true anymore. Rip away my ego.

Like the weather, our life has fine, cloudy, rainy, or snowy days but whatever the weather for the day, 'wanting to have a piss' is reality-as-it-is. (Sorry for the metaphor. I just happened to have an urge to go to the toilet right that moment.) Allowing truth to be truth, I finish urinating, and then I no longer have any urge - e.g. the truth of that moment disappears, and I move on in the grandeur of emptiness, which is spontaneous, flowing and transforming to the next moment. I see the green bamboo from the window, and marvel at its beauty. That bamboo isn't man-made. It is a creation of nature. Likewise, I, Azusa Kakeno, also belong to nature. Nature gives me everything I need, and nature assigns my role in this world.

Azusa! Live every moment in mu and be totally open to new possibilities. Remember?! Just like when you started studying to become a qualified tax accountant.

Clouds in the sky constantly change their form; even if a part of a cloud insisted on remaining fixed in one place, it wouldn't be feasible. Life is exactly the same.

However, we are susceptible to attachments of all sorts - social status, role, authority, schooling, money, possessions, theory, beliefs, on and on. As if validating our self-worth, we imprint the information of our attachments in our consciousness and use them as our own power source to constantly pass judgments on others. Unseemly 'as it is', I have not quite broken away from that pattern of behavior. But at least I am far more aware of my unattractive side. My sincere thanks to Roshi for heightening my self-awareness. I am truly grateful to him.

As I went deeper into zazen, my body and mind became focused on what I needed to do right this moment - just pursue each single breath scrupulously. I was experiencing a stream of insights, but I let them go immediately and returned to one-pointed inhalation and exhalation.

We humans are all given a certain number of breaths for the whole of our lifetime. Regardless of whether we are conscious of this gift or not, we die when we have consumed our ration. The greatest happiness lies in just breathing. The greatest happiness lies in just taking this one step. The greatest happiness lies in just drinking and eating. The greatest happiness lies in just pissing, just shitting. But most people look for the greatest happiness somewhere else, while they already have it with them right here. Only when we gain insight into this cardinal truth does the whole world of truth start to reveal itself.

Whatever arose in my zazen - a thought or sensation - disappeared quietly and I came back to each single breath. I went deeper and deeper and felt as if my entire being was orchestrated into breathing.

We are often caught up with our attachments to money and material things. But money cannot buy a single breath. Simply inhale, complete. Then, exhale and complete. One truth completed surrenders itself to another truth. Truth is revealed in just being as is. I realized for the first time that the only permanence that existed was this perpetual cycle of a beginning being an ending; an ending, another new beginning. It was profoundly peaceful to embody this eternal flow.

Whether we are humans or plants, we are all like air. Yes, air. All things are essentially empty, like air. What we perceive as phenomenal existence is insubstantial. It is nothing more than a constellation of karma. Yes, I was touching the world of the Great Prajna Paramita Heart Sutra. Tears welled up as another layer of my consciousness was lifted. I am not maudlin. It was just that each time a layer of consciousness was stripped off and I came closer to my essence, I was struck with a sense of liberation, inspiration, wonder, and I guess, gratitude. And I ended up in tears.

There were three guests for dinner but I just ate without even greeting them. I was absorbed in the world of ku where all sentient beings are essentially insubstantial; I felt like a monk who had just become enlightened. I told myself I must not indulge in the delirium of joy. I must not leave space for anything other than just eating. But the truth was, even if I had been told to leave some space, I still wouldn't have been able to do it. The world of ku is well beyond the dichotomy of either leaving or not leaving space. All of us had come to Roshi to experience 'just being'. Compared with the vital importance of that, the trivial affairs of the external world really did not matter.

As I finished eating, I said to myself, 'I wish I had a cup of tea now.' The moment I thought about this I was rebuked by Roshi.

"Ms. Kakeno, watch out! Your attention is drifting. You are about to move into full-fledged practice. You must not slacken your concentration on the path. Imbecile!"

How on earth could he always catch me out? He is incredibly quick and strict.

I was assigned to clean up the kitchen. I washed the rice bowls single-mindedly - a very rewarding experience because it was on-the-job practice; I could grasp the moment when my attention was diverted for other thoughts, and immediately leave them behind, while continuing to wash dishes.

Yes, it's only when our minds are drifting that we break dishes.

"Ms. Kakeno, it's a pity you have to leave on the twenty-ninth of December, while you are making such good progress. Why don't you stay longer, do midnight zazen on New Year's Eve, and return on New Year's Day?" said Roshi.

Great idea! I agreed on the spot. I had to be back on the second of January as I was expecting guests that day. But other than that, I was more than happy to give up my New Year holiday for zazen; the holiday did not mean much compared to the richness of being that I was experiencing through Zen practice.

Fifth Day

I woke up at 4:30 a.m. I was finally getting used to Seminary life without heating. Under a sky full of stars and crunching frost, I walked down the steep hill from the Seminary to the main hall of the temple to attend the morning service starting at 6 a.m. It was very dark and hard to believe that in forty minutes it would be daybreak.

The striking feature of the main hall in a Zen temple is its plain simplicity matching the austerity of Zen.

All the students, between five and ten of us each day, chanted the sutras with heart and soul. In spite of many unfamiliar words, it was deeply nourishing for me to chant; as my mind became more focused, with greater clarity, I was more open to appreciate the richness and depth of the world depicted in the sutras.

I think hymns are also beautiful and inspiring. But the rather monotonous melody of sutra chanting, with almost no emotional expression, definitely engenders solemnity, each intoning voice a manifestation of the natural essence of each person. With our voices flowing together through the huge, bare hall, the slow and serene rhythm of chanting creates a powerful resonance. It evokes pure beingness, making me ever more open and peaceful and rising into infinitely larger realms of no-thing.

The solemn morning service ended with three prostrations, casting the whole body away. The hall with no lights was like a huge cave - its profound quietness was echoed in the stillness of my mind, which highlighted the luminosity of soul like a bright diamond in the dark.

Honoring the diamond of my Buddha-nature, I was more meticulous than ever taking each step. Out of the main hall, the Seto Inland Sea loomed dimly. The Zen temple stood grave and enigmatic against the dark mountains. Not even a bird was awake. In this profound stillness, the 'clack-clack' of wooden sandals, for which I always had a special affinity, took me into an ever deeper realm.

Roshi was waiting for me on the hill to the Seminary. I was instantly on guard.

"Ms. Kakeno, how many steps were there up to this point?"

"...."

"How many steps did it take you to get here?"

Oops! Goodness! Too late! My mind was not wholly on each single step but diverted, busily searching for the answer. But the moment I realized I was lax, I brought my focus back to my footsteps.

"How many steps were there up to this point?" Roshi repeated in a somewhat sharp tone.

"One step," I said. This was clear evidence that I had presented the meaning of 'step' on the level of consciousness, but not of undivided practice. Oops! I then took a step immediately. Although I was dumfounded by his unexpected questioning, I recognized the inadequacy of what I had done, and my body had spontaneously responded by taking a step. Not spot on, but still I should say I made some progress.

Roshi gave no comment to my delayed response, and I took his silence as tacit approval. I was glad at least he did not say "No!"

In the brief time before breakfast, I decided to visit Roshi's room to discuss the Dharma. There I saw a most striking scene.

Roshi was bowing down before the pictures of his teachers, hung in the tokonoma, in exactly the same dignified manner as he did during the morning service. Clearly, his teachers were in the room; whether they were alive or not, Roshi's reverence for them remained vividly alive.

Indeed, Roshi's prostration was the infinite heart, manifested through ritual. Seeing this, I followed Roshi and bowed down before them, too. I had no other choice. This small episode persuaded me that the authenticity of any religion had its origin in the authenticity of spirit.

Later, Roshi sat at his table, swiftly preparing a cup of gyokuro, refined green tea, for me. He shook a tiny teapot to get the last drop of tea into the cup. He did it again and again, and I smiled spontaneously, no-thing in my mind.

"Amazing, isn't it? You are making good progress," said Roshi.

He was right. I had not the slightest idea what Roshi saw in me now. I had not intended to smile. I had no mind, no emotion. So there was no 'I' to be the subject of his observation. I was just smiling because of the mystery of communion with Roshi; each movement Roshi made in serving tea felt so intimate - as if I was doing it.

Previously, I would have been startled by his comment. Perhaps Roshi knew exactly why I smiled and tested me with his comment. Anyway, there was no question that his eyes were penetrating and saw into the state of my internal world, moment by moment.

"To the extent that the feeling of separateness disappears, you can understand there is actually no gap between self and others. What you are experiencing now is the world of one ku mind meeting another ku mind, the original unity of self and others. You experienced that sense of oneness just now, the sense that you were shaking the teapot. You have reached the point where you can experience that unity.

When you are completely cleared of your foggy mind, you can awaken to your pure beingness – the world exactly as it is, the world that is available for every person.

Remember, the purpose of practice is to awaken! Give all your heart and soul to your practice," said Roshi, glaring at me.

This time I clearly understood what he was telling me. Every time I listened to his Dharma talk, there was increasing clarity and certainty.

"Ego, by its nature, invites confrontation and conflict. Zen practice is solely focused to dissolve your ego, the source of separateness and opposition."

When I had first heard this, I could not fully appreciate his remark. I thought there should be more to persevering with this arduous practice than just obliterating one's ego.

Now it was different. I knew from my heart of hearts that was it. It was both uplifting and deepening to listen to the same talk again. I was no longer resisting, questioning, or criticizing. I just listened.

That way, his talk was potent purification for my soul in the immediate present. This must be the ego-less state of mind in which two minds have mutual direct access. I realized that dissolution of the boundary that separated my small self from the outside world engendered the best possible milieu for the human psyche to function. Our minds can operate in the depth that transcends the apparent differences of personality and disposition.

No-mind must be the state of complete openness. No-mind must be the instant of surrendering all my resistance. No-mind must rest in the present, free from the memory of the past and the anticipation of the future. How amazing that these insights came to me naturally! Dropping the ego seemed to be the key for a larger life.

"Roshi, all was ku," I reported. Needless to say, Roshi already knew.

"Exactly. But simply having knowledge of it does not give you any real strength. You need to embody the experience of being ku yourself. Unless you die to yourself thoroughly and transmute your knowledge into your own experience, your understanding is not authentic," said Roshi, again with glaring eyes.

Even Roshi's fierce look did not affect me anymore. It was not because I had become blunted or diminished my intellectual alertness; rather, it was because I had acquired the strength to see things exactly as they were through zazen. No longer did I imagine his piercing look was a threat to me.

I realized that a large part of my day-to-day mental activity had been quite destructive, imagining and reacting to my own imagination, instead of accepting and dealing with reality 'as it is'. The truth was that once delusions started to breed more delusions, their sweeping power and speed were beyond the reach of my intellect to contain. I could now appreciate why zazen must be central to my life.

In the course of our dialogue, Roshi, out of the blue, assigned me an extremely important mission. I am not ready to talk about it at this stage. But the mission felt too big for me.

In tears I asked Roshi, "How am I going to do it?"

"I know you can do it." was his simple answer.

If it was meant to be my mission, I had no choice but to accept my responsibility and just do it. No time for tears. After a while, I felt energized, with a new sense of motivation welling up.

After breakfast, I cleaned up the zendo; I was mindful to remove the dust from each piece of mesh of the tatami mat. A sense of serenity and clarity pervaded as I swept, then wiped the floor with a wet cloth. I said to myself, 'I will cherish this sense of bliss, whenever I do cleaning from now on.'

Previously, I had no idea that cleaning could bring me such happiness. I relished the unlimited sense of unity as the skin of separation fell away.

At 9:30 a.m. I went into the zendo. The moment I lit an incense stick, I realized its smoke simply ascended without any striving. The meandering smoke eventually disappeared into the air. Up to that moment, I had never given serious thought to smoke rising; I had taken it for granted. ut the stream of smoke I was gazing at in the zendo clearly had its own will, endowed by nature. It even had its own personality. The smoke was alive, moving, definitely existing.

The smoke of the incense stick continued to merge into the air, and when it disappeared, only the ashes remained. The mystery was that the ashes that were left behind had their own natural place, too, an irrefutable reason to just be there. They were not the end, the waste from a burnt-out stick of incense.

I was doing zazen on a tatami mat. The tatami mat could not become human, and vice versa, a human could not become tatami, no matter how much they wished to interchange their being. Tatami existed as tatami, human as human. The truth was that they were simply the way they were from the beginning.

The universe in which we live is already the world of truth. Delusion and resulting anguish arise only because of arbitrary human constructs.

After lunch, Roshi asked, "Ms. Kakeno, would the ratio of random thoughts to your focus on breathing be about fifty-fifty?"

"..." It was a strange way of asking a question.

"I assume your attention on the breath lasts longer than your random thoughts. You can drop thoughts now, can't you?"

"Yes."

I knew something was going to happen, but I answered anyway. Sure enough, my zazen after lunch was bombarded with ceaseless waves of thoughts. Now I understood what Roshi's question was pointing to! Goodness me! I ran away, and there fell into another ambush of thoughts. I purposely moved away, and there they were, waiting again. By the time I cut off one thought, I was already assailed by another. It seemed that nothing could be done.

I was desperate. In the end, I tried tilting my head, blowing those thoughts up to the ceiling, but all in vain; the raging thoughts were always poised to attack again. At last I gave in and decided to have a break.

Although that was the most disturbing battle ever, I knew I could find a way through. At 3:30 p.m. I went to the kitchen and had a cup of hot water so I could shift my modus operandi to fighting off thoughts.

Refreshed, I went back to the zendo, this time determined to win the battle. Good gracious! As I sat, huge armies of thoughts, much larger than before, stampeded me, while laying a trap on every pathway of my breathing. I had given in earlier, but that was by no means a withdrawal. I had confidence that my spiritual strength would sustain me and, no matter how huge the armies, they could not inflict decisive damage.

At around 5 p.m. I finally came out of the battle. I had to admit that my understanding of 'all is emptiness' was still very shallow. The reality was the world of delusion had not lost its potency, but was only in hiding, waiting for the chance to overtake me at any time.

It was as if my higher consciousness was whispering to me, 'You only experienced a glimpse of realization, nothing to be elated about. The real, challenging part of your practice is yet to come.' Exhausted and confused, I broke down again.

How many times had I cried since I came to the Seminary? One of my constant thoughts was about my future mission and the conflict between my yearning to live up to my mission and the insurmountable difficulty which I anticipated on the way.

It was hard to explain why I was wailing. It only made sense to me. Tears kept streaming down as I thought about the mission Roshi had hammered into my mind. But it was both refreshing and nourishing to be able to just cry, either because I was immersed in the world of 'tada,' just, simply, only, or else I intuitively felt crying was acceptable at Shorinkutsu Seminary.

Without any warning, someone turned the light on in the zendo. Again I had an insight. If I kept my eyes closed, I would not be able to see anything, even with the light on. That was exactly what happened to us in the world of mumyo.

In our daily life, our mind's eyes remain closed in just the same way as we shut our eyes, so we cannot see the truth and the beauty that the world is offering to us. This insight was like strong lightening passing through my whole body. Locked in our blindness, we still pretend to see the infinity of the universe. No wonder we constantly have problems and cannot resolve them, because we are not seeing.

The light illuminates all, without any bias. If I can have that gift of the mind's eye, I vow to make the right use of it, with total openness and humility.

Bodai-shin is the mind that seeks the path, the mind that strives to cultivate self, the mind that perseveres. If I place bodai-shin at the heart of my practice and pursue my practice, I know I can get there. I wish to make my best effort - in total openness and humility.

I believe the ultimate state of the human mind is bodai-shin. Roshi once said if we apply bodai-shin single-mindedly, then hell can be transformed into nirvana. I have faith in my bodai-shin which gives me enormous strength. Roshi, I ask for your compassionate guidance. I promise to be a ball of bodai-shin.

Sixth Day

At 5 a.m. I started to sit in the zendo.

But now, suddenly, the whole experience of zazen, which had been so satisfying, became an infuriating exercise.

That insensitive Mr. S! I wanted to grab him and give him a good slap. 'Students in the zendo need to respect a few rules. It is common sense boy. If you are going to continue that sickening sighing in the zendo, get out! Furthermore, you're always going in and out of the zendo, running around. I am fed up with your noisy footsteps!'

My anger was inflamed; I felt as if Mr. S's insensitive behavior was jeopardizing the serenity I had found. I was appalled by the intensity of my uncontrollable rage - an emotion I rarely experienced. Then I recalled that Mr. S was scheduled to leave the Seminary today. 'Let's put up with him a few more hours. This must be part of some challenging practice assigned to me,' I worked hard in my zazen so I could accept this trial with appreciation.

At supper time, I heard that Mr. S had changed his mind and was now going to stay on. Behind his tempestuous behavior must have been a painful internal struggle. Now he had finally found some focus in his practice, and leaving the Seminary at this stage would be out of the question. That was excellent. I was very pleased for him.

"If you continue your practice," I said to Mr. S, "you must honor some minimum rules in the zendo. I have been so angry with you. I haven't felt such strong anger as this for many years." The words flowed out of me.

Roshi asked, "Is the anger still there?"

I searched my mind, but there was no trace of it, just a wondrous lightness and freshness.

"You cleared it completely. Your anger was not personal but arose from the Dharma. The Dharma made you speak that way to Mr. S for his own sake and for the sake of all of us. The Dharma shouted at him through you." Thus I learned that anger could also result from practicing the Dharma.

Seventh Day

This morning I tried to recall the anger I had felt with Mr. S yesterday. Then I had thought his behavior was absolutely inexcusable. But now I was clean and clear, with no vestige of anger, almost to the point of asking myself, 'Was I really infuriated last night?' The power to chop off past and future must be a manifestation of the Dharma at work. Though expressing anger, I was not controlled by it. This is how we all aspire to function.

Zazen in the afternoon was focused just on each breath. My body and mind were nothing but bodai-shin. I strove fiercely and went into deep concentration.

"Would you mind giving us a hand to help with supper?" one of the monks came to ask me in the zendo.

As I stepped into the kitchen, I was flabbergasted to see a huge octopus that had just arrived as someone's gift. It was still alive in a pot as big as a baby's bathtub, its enormous legs moving in the boiling water. No wonder even the veteran monk found it hard to handle all by himself. I quickly picked up a stick and held the octopus under the water, until it no longer moved. I made an effort to just see it and hoped the octopus had left this life in peace.

A meal for eight people, including some guests, was soon ready, and we all sat around the table to eat. With some sake served for the first time, a lively conversation went back and forth. In the midst of the feast, however, my whole body was dying to return to the zendo.

At last, I begged Roshi, "Would you please excuse me? I'd like to go back to the zendo now. I really want to do zazen. I cannot resist it."

"Ms. Kakeno, at last your true bodai-shin is being evoked, isn't it?"

"Yes!"

Initially, I had tried to be respectful and patient until the dinner was over. But my body could not wait any longer. Not that I was driven by a sense of intense urgency, but I was anxious to enter the state of mind that I had coveted for so long. I was replete and I could not drink anyway so it was not worth sitting around the table. And above all, I had come here to practice.

I dedicated myself to zazen well past midnight.

The wind was strong outside. An empty bucket went clank-clank from time to time, but the sounds were sucked into deep silence again.

Another pleasurable sound was the rustling of leaves. How refreshing nature was; the simpler and more spontaneous I grew the more open I was to its nourishing energy.

I sank into zazen, deeper than ever. My body had transformed into a hollow through which breath flowed right through - in and out. I lost the sense of my body as a boundary. I no longer had a stomach or intestines. The sound of each single moment went right through me, and I became the sound. I melted away with each breath into the universe. No trace of anything left behind. I would report this to Roshi tomorrow. No, he would already know it anyway.

I said to myself, 'Treat yourself with the utmost respect. And at the same time let yourself go each day. You are practicing so you can totally believe in yourself.'

Eighth Day

This morning I read a poster on the wall in the room next to mine.

'Tada' - just being - is the Buddha's world, beyond thought. Your existence keeps unfolding in relationship to endlessly changing conditions. Knowing you will die anyway; strive to practice now with your heart and soul. Original Self is whole in itself. Musing over this and that are nothing but impediments. Diligence! Diligence! Your diligent application is the manifestation of your bodai-shin. Strive scrupulously to let your thoughts go. That is all there is to the practice. Kaatz! Kaatz!

While thinking of stopping to think, still thoughts keep arising. How pathetic that you keep thinking not to think!

Tips for sesshin

1. Empty your mind and always act in accordance with the Dharma.
2. Be mindful of every movement. Live wholly in the present.

3. Refrain from chatting. Be careful of not disturbing the concentration of other students' practice.
4. Zazen is the life of the Buddha and the masters of old. Devote yourself thoroughly to zazen in the zendo.
5. Have a private interview or dokusan with Roshi at any time you have a question.

After having practiced for a few days, it was much easier to appreciate the message in the poster than before.

I loved Roshi's vivid calligraphy.

I went into the zendo.

To belittle myself and say 'I am just another ordinary person' would be a real insult to this solid sense of presence I was experiencing in zazen. Breathing was naturally guiding me to being, and that being-as-I-am was truly a miracle.

Time and time again, insights rose up in my mind. In contrast to the process of step-by-step thinking, they emerged spontaneously and helped me to understand the essence of highly abstract ideas in a flash. These insights most likely emerged because they were already ingrained in me.

"Soon you will be sweating blood with your insights. Ms. Kakeno, you must not acknowledge and validate your insights during zazen," Roshi had said earlier.

This must be exactly what he intimated. But I was fascinated by my seemingly limitless insights, illuminating one sophisticated idea after another. Having my own insights was a far more concrete and valuable experience than, for instance, reading hundreds of philosophy books and extracting their keywords.

Suddenly it occurred to me that I had lost track of simple breathing.

Why?

It had been going extremely smoothly up to now. I knew why. It was because I was enthralled with my insights. What a fiasco!

Why was it then that I could not go back to steady breathing?

The answer was not hard to find. It was because I was trying to manipulate my breathing. That was wrong. Breathing was teaching me everything I needed to know. Just breathing and only breathing was all I needed to do. As simple as that. But my mind was distracted first by my insights and by then trying to impose them on reality. I told myself to leave them behind.

I must admit that the full meaning of Roshi's comments often went unappreciated until I became entrapped in the very situation he predicted.

Still, they were useful guidance. Without them, I would remain forever confused with my own reasoning, let alone my own rationalizations.

I felt sleepy. It's all very well to say drowsiness is a natural phenomenon, but it's very hard to fight.

Roshi always said, "Lazy people would never bother to come all the way to do zazen here. When you are very sleepy, you must be tired. Go and have a short sleep. You will be amazed with your progress in zazen afterwards."

It was wonderful that Roshi encouraged us to be gentle on ourselves and flow naturally, without straining our body.

Later in the morning I had about one hour of sleep. After this, I went back to the zendo.

This time zazen was smooth. Each of my breaths was clear, distinct, and in the moment. Let it be.

Let it be.

When thoroughly focused on each breath, it was the breath that was guiding and nourishing me. I now began to understand the infinitely profound meaning of Roshi's remark - "Be totally mindful of each single breath." Yes. I was on the right track.

Kaizoji, Roshi's temple, was about five minutes by car from the Seminary. All of us went there in the afternoon for a major year-end clean-up. The scenery of the Seto Inland Sea from Kaizoji was strikingly beautiful. There was no boundary between myself and the scenery as I merged into its freshness.

Although the Seto-Inland Sea looked calm, I was told the currents were very strong. The layers of mountains across the Sea belonged to Ehime Prefecture, Shikoku Island. Although once famous as the historic site of a spectacular battlefield, the whole area was infinitely peaceful, and I hoped it would always remain so.

I was assigned to clean up the main hall and the area behind the hall. I wiped scrupulously with a wet cloth; the whole exercise was a most fulfilling experience. I said to myself that I must cherish this.

The bun with bean-jam filling we had after the clean-up was so delicious that I will not forget it for the rest of my life.

From 5 p.m. I did zazen in the zendo.

My breathing took me into deeper stillness. It moved from my belly, chest, throat, nose, eyes and forehead to the crown of my head. When I let it be, the breathing was infinitely calm. Two hours went quickly.

Knowing the difficult mission ahead of me, Roshi suggested I stay and continue my practice.

At dinner, he said, "Ms. Kakeno, you will be all on your own on New

Year's Day, if you return tomorrow. You will not have any food. The kitchen will be cold. How about staying here a couple more days?"

I was grateful for his thoughtful offer. I also wanted to make the best of this opportunity and my fortunate encounter with Roshi. So I tried to contact the guests who were coming to visit my house on the second of January, but there was no way I could. Inevitably, I had to leave on the first. But I had Roshi's permission to come and practice zazen for three days every month, starting from January.

After dinner I went to Roshi's room.

He said, "After you go back make sure to allocate time for zazen every morning and night. It does not have to be long but it should be absolutely high quality zazen. Concentrate as if your life is at stake. Deepen the current state of openness that latches onto nothing. Then your sharpened intellect will help you see the suchness of things around you. It will be an amazing experience for you."

He spoke no more. And I did not ask any more questions, though I knew he foresaw everything about me.

His rigorous, unspoken message to me was 'what was the use of hearing and having word
knowledge?' Unless I had insight through my immediate experience, I could not grasp the true nature of reality anyway. If I pursued 'just being in the present and that only,' I would be able to access the essential for sure. But the only way I would get there was through my own effort.

Fortunately, diligent application and self-improvement had been built into me since my childhood and had become second-nature. This helped me immensely.

I realized living in the moment itself was truly a sacred experience; living in the moment required no inconsequential rationalizations to validate its sacredness. Every experience was vibrant, and nothing was wasted. It felt great to be alive.

I was happy Roshi listened and nodded to each of my remarks.

Perhaps because of the few cups of fine gyokuro tea Roshi served me and the nap I had during the day, I was wide awake and could not sleep that night. Usually in a similar situation, I would become too eager to sleep and attempt a few techniques in vain. But not this time. The only thing I did was pursuing each breath with tranquility of mind and let my breathing take care of the rest. I was grateful once again for being taught the right way to practice.

But my breathing could do nothing to block the draught coming into the futon, so I pulled it over my head. Contented, thankful for everything and trusting tomorrow would be a happy day, I eventually fell into a deep sleep.

Ninth Day (the thirty-first of December)

I woke up at 4:30 a.m. At last, the final day of the year had arrived.

Could I have anticipated my present practice twelve months ago? No. Absolutely not. This was innen-muryo at work — meaning an innumerable succession of incidents taking place depending on countless direct and indirect causes, that had led to my practice right this moment. In both time and space, the universe is boundless, and everything is interrelated. Roshi, you are quite right, when you say "How could you dare claim that this infinite vastness is knowable through your limited scope of mind; you have enough trouble knowing who you are, let alone the working of the universe."

Above anything else, I must do zazen. I was in the zendo by 4:50a.m. The temperature was well below zero.

Soon I brought my focus back to a single breath.

Morning service down at the temple was cancelled; instead, we were told to continue zazen. Most likely, the change was made so I could sit longer. Challenging thoughts were rising in relation to my mission. I gave no thought about how to address them. I trusted I could handle them in time. I could now cut off my thoughts without any difficulty. But still, noises were noises. I thought Roshi's penetrating eyes had caught me thinking, and that was why he extended the time for zazen this morning. Oh! This thought itself was another random thought! Stop! Stop thinking!

Suddenly all thoughts were gone.

There was no way I could afford stop zazen now.

My whole self was absorbed in a single breath, in a single moment.

After breakfast, we spent three more hours doing the year-end clean-up for the Seminary. Then, I went back to the zendo at 11 a.m. It was a practice of ease - a practice of playfulness and delight.

The breath was me. I was the breath. Both my breath and I were immersed in the world of mu. This must be the ultimate crux of Zen practice.

Zazen in the afternoon was not as equanimous as the morning zazen; perhaps my eagerness to experience the same degree of serenity had become an attachment, and thus a hindrance.

That evening I took a bath. Since I had come to the Seminary, all my senses had expanded enormously and I particularly relished bathing. I sank my body into it. The water was lukewarm, and it was too cold to get out of the bathtub. I wanted someone to burn more firewood to boil water. I was naked and unsure of whether to ask for it. But what about the next bather?

And what if I caught cold? For these two reasons, I shouted, "Excuse me! The water is too cold." Fortunately there was someone outside, but it took time to heat up enough water.

"Is it getting warmer?" the voice asked from outside.

"No! No improvement at all!" I shouted back with unintended honesty.

Staying in the lukewarm bath longer than usual, however, helped keep my body warm after getting out of the bath.

A healthy tension pervaded the whole Seminary that evening. With the last minute of the year 1995 nearing, each one of us felt a special need to go deep into ourselves and made an extra effort.

At 7:00 p.m. I went back to the zendo. I applied myself fervently and focused on each breath. A powerful momentum was building up with thirteen of us sitting intently. Mr S's progress had been especially remarkable. He had turned into a different person. There was more clarity and even a sort of dignity in his presence now.

Roshi's compassion for Mr S was immeasurably deep. Roshi guided him inch by inch, while Mr S slowly recovered from his pathological behavior. He used to scream and cry in the zendo; his noisy footsteps and unpleasant sighing had been extremely disruptive to other sitters. Now he had almost turned into a healthy Zen student.

Mr. S arrived at the Seminary five days earlier than me, and I knew nothing of how he was then. What I witnessed was a highly intelligent young man writhing in excruciating pain. How distressing it must have been to find himself incapable of handling ordinary life.

According to Mr. S, he had searched for his spiritual salvation in countless religions. The history of his journey was staggering, including his devotion to that notorious Aum Supreme Sect. He had wandered from religion to religion and went as far as India and Tibet. Possessed by an inner drive, he had been making an extraordinary effort. Inoue Roshi was his last resort. He trusted Roshi and struggled to stay in the practice. A whole spectrum of modern medicine, including counseling, had failed to bring him back his wholesome state of mind. Now, Zen practice was offering a process for saving himself and was eliciting real change in him. I was often touched by his improvements.

Unlike many men of religion, Roshi has an extraordinary analytic mind and can articulate his observations in logical steps. Mobilizing these strengths, Roshi patiently kept unraveling each of Mr. S's twisted brain circuits, which had been overloaded with excessive and incoherent pieces of knowledge.

"Mr. S, I haven't had a challenging student like yourself for quite a while.

Interacting with you alone is the equivalent of teaching well over ten Zen students. But I also give you credit for your perseverance and diligence. You have been really gutsy. Stick with me and push yourself through under my guidance.

I assure you, you will get well," Roshi continued. "Mr. S, don't expect there are people 'out there' who can save you. Most importantly, there isn't anyone who can penetrate your extremely complex and distorted view of reality. When a student makes a promise to me and breaks it, usually the best solution is to expel him or her from the Seminary. It is especially important to do this for the sake of other striving students. However, I could not abandon you when you broke your promise. I could not let you go without giving you an opportunity for your mind to start softening. Because I know you are a highly intelligent, serious, honest, and tenacious young man."

Roshi was totally committed to offer his best guidance to Mr. S. His commitment arose from his compassion to care for and nourish each person.

One morning, rather unusually, Roshi began talking in front of everyone during zazen. "Mr. S, you have to respect your need for sleep. Up to now, the disorder of your autonomic nervous system has kept you over-stimulated around the clock. You could neither have a good sleep nor be alert. You were always tired and could not get rid of your fatigue. But now that your body and mind are starting to be in tune, you can have a deep sleep. Enjoy it thoroughly. Now the alternate states of relaxation and healthy tension will become more distinct allowing your cerebrum to rest accordingly. As a result, your perceptiveness will grow sharper; you will be in control of your behaviorbehavior through your own consciousness. So, have a good sleep whenever you can."

That was Roshi's guidance when Mr. S was dozing off in his zazen. In a similar situation, an average Zen teacher would have hit him hard with the kyosaku with the intention of awakening him from his torpor. And this would have further shattered his self-esteem and hardened his already distorted mind.

'Mr. S, hang in there. You will genuinely experience your own salvation here,' I silently sent my encouragement to him, feeling like a mother.

A couple days later, Roshi praised his progress with gentle humor, while pretending to look serious. "Mr S, you have evolved from reptile to primate. But still, dogs and cats have a lot to teach you. They do not think of their death; they are free from any anxiety and they just live in response to the present. Our imaginings are the product of human intellect. Our imaginings can frighten us. But it is also through human intellect that we anticipate the consequences of our behavior. Foreseeing undesirable consequences, we can consciously choose a set of behaviors to prevent this from happening. But you haven't quite reached the stage of understanding the consequences of your own actions. Your brain circuits need a few more steps to qualify you as fully human. At least you are finished with your reptilian stage of evolution, a period of total separation from what goes on around you."

With his use of humorous metaphor, Roshi encouraged greater self-awareness in Mr. S. His stooped posture became upright. Previously when he held chopsticks and a bowl of rice, he looked exactly like a chimpanzee - with no trace of any human intelligence. Now he was eating with grace. I had witnessed Roshi's commitment in guiding Mr. S so that he could regain his sense of authority.

Nothing pleased me more than seeing Mr. S able to start the new year afresh, as the new person he had become through practice. Now he could truly appreciate the ordinariness of each day, no matter how simple or routine.

Close to midnight, the bell of Shounji Temple began to ring. Just that sound 'boom'.

Twelve o'clock - the moment the new calendar year started. I had no emotion. Temple bells all over Japan rang one hundred and eight times simultaneously to signal the end of the old year and the coming of the new. This traditional ritual, I think, is important as it serves to draw a line between the ending and beginning of time, which, otherwise, would just be a continuation of another day. Five hours of zazen went in a flash. I must have sunk into zazen.

'Boom, boom, boom.'

'Boom' and I merged into oneness; 'boom' was my being, and with another 'boom', my being was emerging again.

Roshi suddenly broke the silence of zazen and said, "For those who wish to take this opportunity to ring the bell, please feel free to do so."

I gathered that a few students had left the zendo to ring the bell. As for myself, I wanted to stay and relish the experience of my whole being participating in the sound of 'boom'. But contrary to my intention, I became sleepy and dozed off. Without a moment's delay, Roshi clouted me with the kyosaku.

Crack! Oh, boy! It hurt, especially on my left shoulder. I would probably develop a big blue bruise there. But I was pleased I had no emotion about it.

At 1:30 a.m. the small bell rang to signal the end of zazen. We prostrated to the old teachers, bowed down to Roshi, and exchanged greetings ourselves. Then we gathered in the dining room. It was packed with people joining our feast for the new year. It must have taken lots of time and effort to prepare this gorgeous meal. In my heart, I bowed to the people who had cooked for us.

"Happy New Year!" We all toasted.

There was plenty of sake and beer together with a big hot-pot cooked at the table. The leeks in the hot-pot were beautiful. Mr. I, who was sitting with us, grew them on his farm. Their exquisite taste was truly a reflection of his loving care. I spontaneously expressed my thanks to him.

It was 3:30 a.m. when we finished the clean-up and went to sleep. And one hour later, at 4:30 a.m. we were up again. In no time, I was ready to go back to the zendo as I had not even taken my jumper off to sleep. I started my zazen at 4:45 a.m.

A few people sounded as if they had fallen asleep during zazen. I heard the regular breathing of sleeping sitters - ssss, ssss, ssss. Though admittedly sleepy, I kept telling myself I must stay awake.

But soon my attention drifted away from my breathing and was lured by the sleepers' breathing.

Having had only one hour of sleep that was my strange first period of zazen of the New Year. The high spirits of the sitters were nonetheless quite inspiring. Even with some occasional nodding off, their fierce determination to sit through to the dawn of the first day of the year was contagious.

Roshi would have probably shouted at us, if he was with us. "Sleepy zazen is not effective. Don't do it! Go back to your room and have a good sleep!"

At 8:00 a.m. we had a bowl of zohni, a traditional New Year's breakfast of rice cakes boiled in soup, my favorite food.

After breakfast, Roshi and all the other students went down to Kaizoji-Temple for the New Years' service. I was the only one left in the zendo.

Having the zendo all to myself, my New Year zazen was invigorating.

I totally forgot myself in the act of breathing. Had anyone told me to divert my attention from breathing, it would not have been possible. I was just breathing, nothing else.

Suddenly, I heard a voice, "Ms. Kakeno!" It was Mr. Yusetsu calling me from outside.

"We are going to have lunch at Kaizoji. Please come and join us. We will drive you down to the station so you can catch the 2:53 p.m. train," said Mr. Yusetsu.

He had come to fetch me. "Thank you."

How thoughtful of them. I quickly changed out of the hakama into my suit. I then brought in the sheet, pillow cover, and kake futon cover that I had hung on the wash line in the morning. My body moved with flowing lightness by its own volition. Every movement was as natural as air flowing. This must be the act of the emptiness emptying.

On the table was a New Year's feast prepared by Roshi's wife and Kaoru, his daughter - my favorite sweet black beans, kidney beans, sunomono, salted herring roe, and sashimi, just to name a few. It was hard to express in words the joy of being surrounded at the table with Zen friends. While enjoying the innumerable number of dishes, we all engaged in lively conversation. Even the landscape felt intimate as I thought I would not be able to see this beautiful scenery of the Seto Inland Sea for the next few weeks.

After having our photos taken in the garden, I left Kaizoji-Temple. Everyone stood by the gate and saw me off. With Kaoru's driving, it took only two minutes to Tadanoumi station, full of people beautifully dressed for the New Year's celebrations. But I had no need for special clothes. I was celebrating the New Year with a completely fresh way of being.

Mr Yusetu, who came with us to the station, handed me Roshi's present, a set of navy blue samue clothes. I figured this was Roshi's encouragement to further my practice.

I bowed to both of them through the train window until they were well out of sight, feeling a surge of deep emotion.

On the train, I was absorbed in just looking at the passing scenery outside. But soon my mind was fantasizing - 'Suppose I buy a villa on such a scenic spot, wouldn't that be great for my relaxation?

Not just that, my employees would be happy to use the facility, too.' The moment I was aware of my delusion, I felt Roshi's glaring eyes and roaring shout, "You, fool! You have already fallen to prey to your delusion!" 'Azusa, stay away from desire and attachment!,' I warned myself.

After changing from the local train to the Shinkansen at Mihara station, I fell into a deep sleep.

I must have been fast asleep throughout the trip. I only woke up as the Shinkansen was nearing Shin-Osaka station. 'Back to the big city - a stifling and at the same time, quite interesting place for me,' I thought with a sense of liberated detachment.

I renewed my absolute commitment to focus on the present and to really follow through each breath in the moment. I worked my way step-by-step through the din and bustle of New Year's Day in Osaka. Nothing interfered with me - neither the streaming crowd nor the incessant arrival and departure of trains.

The diamond of my heart and soul was my only focus; I pledged to honor it.

As I arrived home, I was grateful for all the blessings that life had given me, that Roshi had given me, that practice had given me. I bowed deeply to express my gratitude and appreciation to them all.

What a refreshing leap I had made since the day I left Osaka on the twenty-second of December last year. I gave a big hug to my invisible breath - in the dusk of New Year's Day, 1996.

My Second Sesshin

On the whole my life has not particularly changed since I started Zen practice - at least on the surface, though there is definitely a sense of inner freshness. It feels like the very cells of my body have been rejuvenated through the practice.

Though how I choose to live each day might not be readily visible, I have become more conscious of the absolute preciousness of each day being like a thread woven into my life fabric. This clarity of being alive right this moment is the diamond of my life which I discovered in the practice.

My whole body kept yearning for this unfading clarity of spirit - the fully-oxygenated spirit of here and now. Working on the foundation of my being and pursuing further self-purification became my most pressing needs. And that led me to return to the Seminary for another five days' practice soon after my first sesshin.

If asked what the purpose of my sesshin was, I would categorically say it was to penetrate into the present moment. As Roshi said, "There is no starting point or ending point in Zen practice. To utterly live the present is the beginning and the goal of Zen practice. There is nothing outside the present instant. You become wholly available to that very instant which is extinguished completely in the next instant. You awaken to the reality of things just as they are in the moment, as your mind and body are cast off. The whole point of zazen is to embody this awareness."

I can appreciate this essence of Dharma, at least partly. I would not claim I have fully incorporated it in myself. But I am conscious that the real world has nothing to do with my concepts about it.

My entire life is enlivened; this is all very new to me. A sense of mental and physical well-being permeates; this is derived from my awareness that there is truly nothing other than this moment. I am afraid I cannot fully describe this sense of well-being in words.

With zazen, my mind was becoming infinitely more transparent; filled with child-like joy and wonder. Quiet breathing was guiding me into a sphere of vast openness; the consciousness of 'I' was fading naturally with my breathing. It felt warm and comfortable - nothing to struggle with. This natural state felt like being in my mother's womb.

Having reached my mid-fifties, I should say it was about the right time to pause and reflect on my life passage. So far in my life, thinking ahead and being proactive had been important to my survival. I had committed myself to being fully alert so I could discern what lay ahead.

Surprisingly, the greatest challenge that I was yet to address turned out to be my own being - the self that runs my life. After all, the ultimate question boiled down to this self, and nothing else, for all the choices I made or will make in future.

Moreover, I had some vague uneasiness about my mortal, ephemeral existence. There was no telling when, where, and what kind of tragedy might be waiting for me - in the flickering time of only 70 or 80 years of my life.

Unless I resolved these fundamental questions they would always float in my subconscious, inflicting unnecessary anxiety, fear and suspicion. Not only that, I might end up affecting the life of those around me with my poor judgments and expectations.

Also, I had seen too many cases of those at the helm of their businesses trapped by their obligations and self-interest, who eventually fell into disgrace through illegal conduct. I could not just dismiss them and say that was their problem. I knew I too could be lured into exactly the same trap.

Although I was not fully conscious about it then, this fear might have been my primary motivation in taking up Zen practice under Inoue Roshi.

I had not known zazen could be such a delightful experience until I did my second sesshin. This sesshin left me with a sense of spaciousness, even a tinge of playfulness. I could tune into what others were up to. So, now and again I was tempted to get up to innocent mischief and enjoy a good laugh. It was like wanting to play a game of mind catch ball where the ball I throw is returned to me with equal strength and speed.

But my playfulness did not always work. One day, someone called me on the phone and asked for my address. Teasingly, I said my address was in the cosmos. He was confounded. I wished he had shared my playfulness and said, "Yes, that was what I was after. Please tell me your cosmic address!"

Without openness and playfulness of mind we tend to operate in the mode where things can only be thought of in opposites - gain-or-loss, or friend-or-foe. That is an impoverished way to use our minds, where relationships tend to be brittle and flat.

My second sesshin highlighted this understanding. After a few weeks I went on to do a third sesshin, with hopes for further deepening and refreshing myself.

My Third Sesshin

One cloudy winter morning I stepped once more through the elegant wooden gate. The space beyond the gate - the stone garden, the bamboo shrub, and the modest meditation hall - was serene and settling; this space transcended time and the pettiness of the secular world.

As I went into Roshi's room, I was greeted by those penetrating eyes and the soothing fragrance of an incense stick. Smiling, Roshi made a cup of gyokuro tea for me.

"It is a beautiful cup of tea," I said spontaneously. But the instant I heard myself saying it, I knew something was going to happen.

"How beautiful is beautiful?" asked Roshi.

I was struck dumb by his piercing question. I smiled to conceal my confusion - the typical behavior of a Japanese woman buying time. But I was not flustered.

Roshi pushed me further "Precisely who is it who says the tea is beautiful?"

Roshi's glaring eyes were scary. But I was not constrained by his words. The transparency of my mind helped me to understand the essence of his question. I smiled with renewed confidence. Poised, I stretched my hand, simply picked up a cup of tea, and quietly drank it.

"Oh! Beautiful! Roshi, you make a beautiful cup of tea," I said and stared at him.

I was wholly in the moment. Roshi's questions were checking my being 'just' in the absolute now. A gentle smile returned to Roshi's eyes. That was a good reminder. With all my reverence and feeling of closeness for Roshi, I could never be lax with him, and there was always an underlying healthy tension in every moment shared with him.

On the surface, the trainee monks and students of the Seminary did not appear to be pursuing a rigorous practice, each of them casually doing his or her own task. But this impression only reflected my lack of capacity to penetrate and comprehend what was actually going on. Now I could clearly see each of them striving to be absolutely in the moment.

A typhoon-like gusty wind was blowing outside. But inside the meditation hall, everything had fallen silent. Zazen was guiding me to sink further into tranquility and almost melt into it. Suddenly, the sharp shriek of a bird broke out. But the tranquility remained just the same - I was peaceful.

I looked outside after zazen. The trees -bamboo, chestnut, and camellia - were dancing fiercely in the strong wind, the dynamic movement of their leaves a choreography matching the intense energy of the wind. But I felt profoundly still, undisturbed by the surroundings, struck by the spectacular harmony of nature; trees were dancing, clouds were floating free of all concerns, just scudding with no-mind. In contrast to this harmony in nature, the secular world was full of absurdity, people uptight chasing after big money, possessed by their wealth, or entrapped by their lust.

Our life path is treacherous though it may appear smooth on the surface. Very often, we lose track of the road ahead. It is because our attachment and greed obscure our mind's eye. Many journeys of heroes and heroines in history are good evidence of this. One day their discriminating wisdom starts to dwindle, and they go slowly off the rails.

But in reality it is the other way around; heroes and heroines let themselves go off the rails, and as a consequence, their discriminating wisdom starts losing its power. I often find a similar pattern in the rise and fall of successful business people. They are endowed with discriminating wisdom and given the capacity to persevere and overcome many ordeals. The truth is that wisdom is given to them because life requires them to achieve their mission.

Their success only brings them to the 'starting station' so they now have vehicles to work on the real mission assigned to them in their life journey. But as soon as they arrive at the starting station, they tend to be surrounded by an admiring entourage who are keen to take advantage of their success. All they hear is how brilliant they are. Hubris sets in. Imperceptibly, they begin losing their discriminating wisdom.

They choose that path. They invite their own decline. But pressed by their super-tight schedule, they may not even realize what their choices and its consequences are. Their hectic routine does not afford any quiet time for introspection.

To me the lesson is about reminding myself that I am always at the starting station of my life journey, irrespective of success and any status I might achieve. Without that self-awareness I am bound to go downhill, wasting my effort in futile activities.

The point is to sustain an unceasing aspiration to reach a higher level of consciousness. Although books and lectures by eminent academics might help to refine my intellectual comprehension, which is not sufficient. They may provide the framework for a sophisticated explanation. But it is not a final resolution. It cannot offer non dualistic access to my being. As long as

I resort to my own reasoning, I am constrained by my own perspective. It could be likened to an army marching without knowledge of an ambush up ahead. The limitations of intellectual understanding imply that I will remain inherently restless and unsure of myself, and have reservations about fully trusting and loving others.

Definitely, there is a way to overcome that limitation. It is not about building a broader knowledge base or learning more conceptual frameworks. It is about waking up to the absolute reality of life beyond thought - directly experiencing the realm of pure suchness.

Zazen practice, under the guidance of the right teacher, gives us the discipline of mind to return to the realm of what is. And when we pursue the right path, the step we take will bring about beneficial results in future.

One morning after breakfast I was quietly sitting in the zendo. Just by chance, my eyes caught the corner of the tatami, covered with thick dust. 'What an embarrassment for us Zen students!' I said to myself. The next moment I was up and cleaning with Mr. Kawao who also happened to be in the zendo. We quickly stacked all the mats away; vacuum cleaned, and wiped the whole floor with the wet cloth. Obviously the zendo had not been cleaned for a long time.

I would have thought cleaning should be one of the natural duties of Zen students using the zendo. But there were no rules in Shorinkutsu Seminary except attending the morning service and eating three meals together. Basically, Roshi left us completely free; we could go back to our room for a sleep if we were drowsy, or else we could do zazen as long as we wished - well beyond midnight.

Typical free-spirited Inoue Roshi was not interested in petty formalities. But at the same time he was very strict and demanded that we sustain an unrelenting concentration on 'now' by practicing exactly as he taught.

So it was not because of Seminary rules or because somebody had told us to do a cleanup. Catching sight of the dusty tatami simply flowed into my action of cleaning - with total spontaneity. There was not a trace of myself wanting to be smart and useful. This straight-forwardness of just doing, I thought, must be the essence of the fully functioning, lively mind.

Both Mr. Kawao and I simply cleaned the place, doing what needed to be done. We did not even need to decide who did what. In silence, we just did one thing after the next.

In contrast, the clean-up I had done during the first sesshin with Mr. S was hilarious. He kept asking, "What shall I do?" so I could assign him a certain task. He was clumsy, but did what he was told. If I were to score his performance, I could not give any more than 50%.

Nevertheless, he would come to me again for instruction, asking "What's next?" This went on for the whole time, and his cleaning performance showed no improvement.

As Roshi put it, his mental make-up remained under-developed; it was as if each element in his nervous system was separate and compartmentalized. He could not find any link between the intention to clean and the action; identifying what needed to be cleaned, planning the step-by-step procedures, and acting on them. So, if he were to follow his visual perception, the only thing he would do was to stand by idly. No wonder he found it hard to adapt to an ordinary working environment.

Roshi must have immediately understood the cause of Mr. S's maladaptation. Having worked with Mr. S, I appreciated the enormous patience with which Roshi worked on his fragmented thought process so he could develop the capacity to function in real life situations. Roshi's task was like that of the meticulous weaver finding an almost invisible cut-off thread and mending it carefully to weave it in.

However, when Mr. Kawao was my cleaning partner, it was totally different. We complemented each other; if Mr. Kawao started a certain area, I left it with him and cleaned somewhere else.

We were at ease with each other as reliable partners and thoroughly enjoyed working together. This gave me renewed insight into the requisites for living and working together in harmony.

Needless to say, mutual trust and respect were important. But in no way could we expect to be trusted or respected unless we had that substance within ourselves worthy of trust and respect. Only then, could we mutually recognize the unique attributes of each other and work on developing a complementary relationship. And that was where the spirit of Zen could come into full play; things that need to be done get done, and we move onto the next thing. It all starts from self-cultivation which then allows our effective contribution to the whole. Upon fulfilling our responsibility there, we fade out and move on to the next thing. It is a life of constant renewal, a very simple but refreshing way to live.

My zazen after the clean-up was the best ever; I slipped into deep concentration. I thought I understood what the inscription in the zendo was saying. It read 'If you wish to search for the true meaning of life, experience it through zazen.'

Now that I had learned that cleaning could be an illuminating experience, I seriously began to think of doing a clean-up of my own house. I have always had a cleaner because of my extremely busy schedule.

On the last day of my third sesshin, Roshi gave a Dharma talk after the morning service.

"Zazen is all about resolving our being at the core. That is about seeing ourselves simply as we are - being in touch with life 'as it is'. After all, we are here only for seventy or eighty years. There is no center of life outside our everyday life. Our life here now is an inestimably precious, unique gift.

Everything you see, hear, become aware of, is reality manifesting suchness in the present. What your eye, ear, nose, tongue, body, mind - gen-ni bi zes-shin I - perceive - color, sound, scent, taste, touch, thought - shiki sho ko mi soku ho - is not separate but one and the same. Resolving our being at the core is about gaining a clear awareness of this non dual present.

Roshi said to me: "Ms Kakeno, you have managed to do three sesshins over the past ten weeks. Given your extremely busy life, your effort deserves praise. And you have been making good progress. Keep on practicing, Ms. Kakeno. Your mission will start unfolding in an unexpected way. You are called to serve.

You don't have to bother with when, where, or how you will die. We illuminate the world and disappear when the time comes, like blossoms going with good grace. Birth and death are an integral part of the natural cycle, a part of the one wholeness. And nature-as-simply-'as it is', is the absolute reality beyond human consciousness and emotion. It is much larger than the world of ego claiming its authority over others.

Unless we develop the strength to notice our emotions and thoughts and let them go, we are bound to run into conflict in one way or another. We set ourselves against others, insisting that our reasoning is superior and inviting endless confrontations.

'The know-alls trapped by the question of whether there is Buddha-nature or not, whereas enlightened ones remain uninterested,' is the saying of one old patriarch. Enlightened ones understand that 'this is it'; there is no room for 'is or is not', 'like or dislike', 'true or false'. On the other hand, the 'know-alls' congratulate themselves on the supremacy of their own reasoning. In the end, they can even justify warfare.

So I advise you not to set yourself up as being righteous. Then you are an unbounded self, free to engage with the infinite, boundless realm of the universe. Do not indulge in reasoning. Cut your thoughts off. Penetrate the present moment. These are the essence of the teachings of the Seminary."

Roshi went on, "Ms. Kakeno, greater clarity in the orientation of your life is emerging from your practice. You know what the primary focus is, what is yet lacking, and what is fulfilling in your life. Remember, searching for your own happiness alone is too small a focus. Keep the 'Four Bodhisattva Vows' close to your heart. The many beings are numberless:

I vow to save them, greed, hatred, and ignorance rise endlessly.

I vow to abandon them, Dharma-gates are countless.
I vow to wake to them, Buddha's Way is unsurpassed.
I vow to embody it fully.
(Translation by Roshi Robert Aitken)

We need to look after ourselves, as our body and mind are the agents for realizing the Dharma. And let us all strive to practice and be true to our Bodhai-shin. Everywhere, ominous signs are suggesting the ultimate downfall of human beings.

Can we turn it around? The answer is yes, but only if we start working on ourselves and dissolve our mind habits. There are too many polemicists who only stir up and confuse other people. Don't be distracted by others. Just concentrate on cultivating your Bodhai-shin for the Path."

That was a long sermon, but now that my three sesshins had removed a lot of dross, Roshi's words filtered through my mind with no effort. Ten weeks ago, I had come to the Seminary holding some unresolved questions. Perhaps my questions had been superficial and not that essential to me after all. They had resolved themselves and disappeared completely from my mind during the process of my three sesshins.

Certainly, addressing any problem can be an opportunity for stretching one's mind. However, attaching some meaning to problem-solving itself is an act of reasoning. As long as we are caught up with this and that reason, the mind is inherently restless. The restless mind continues to compare, analyze, and often ends up criticizing others. But what is this mind itself? What is at the very core of the mind?

Inoue Roshi's guidance is exclusively focused on this ultimate core. Roshi points the way so his students can cut through to this core through their own effort.

I must confess that initially my mind was too busy trying to resolve 'my problem,' instead of just listening to Roshi's words.

Had I let my mind go, had I let 'my problem' go, I could have gone deeper into the realm beyond reasoning more quickly. Problems arise from only one source; they arise because the mind gets trapped by the virtual world of our own opinions. What is more, the mind is misled to believe that is the real world. The Zen teacher's role is to awaken students from the self-inflicted delusion of this virtual world.

But, for that fierce battle of deconstructing our false imagery, the right teacher is an absolute requisite; we all need the right teacher, capable of shaking off our intellect with his or her piercing questions. We need to be confounded, not knowing what to say. At times we even need to be condemned and slapped on the cheek a few times - to extricate ourselves from the delusory world.

Just a few hours before leaving the Seminar, Roshi offered a ride to Mr. Kawao and me. As we stepped into his old car, he said to us teasingly, "Now that your minds are clear after sesshin, I would like to stimulate your delusory mind."

Off he drove down a narrow steep road like a roller coaster.

"Watch out! I am going to take you to the place where your mind will be definitely stirred up by your fantasy. Ha! Ha! Ha! Empty your mind and stay focused in your practice. Do not create any fantasy through your thoughts. Engage in just seeing." A weird warning, I thought.

Roshi drove along the scenic coastal road in bright morning sunlight. The numerous small islands made a delicate contrast of light and shadow, the islands overlaying and separating from one another as he drove along. It was hard to just see, but we tried.

Then Roshi turned uphill. 'Hm! This is ominous.' I said to myself.

The further up he went, the more breath-taking the panoramic view of the Seto Inland Sea turned out to be. Excited by its scenic beauty my mind started to lose focus.

Roshi stopped the car at an open space on the edge of a cliff, looking out to sea.

The moment I stepped out of the car, I could no longer resist keeping silent. "Wow! What a beautiful place!" I shouted.

The words rolled out of me. Mr. Kawao was in the same mood. He trotted busily here and there, and I followed him. The place was covered with wild plants. 'It's probably vacant land, without an owner.' As soon as this thought passed through my mind, I was enchanted by a stream of fantasy.

'Wouldn't it be a fantastic place for a holiday house?

What about my company holiday house and the training center?

There wouldn't be any better place; a new hot spring was recently discovered right under this cliff, and a deluxe health retreat is going to be opened here this autumn which will have the best seafood restaurant in the area.'

Roshi must have taken us here knowing exactly how we would behave.

"You two are going to be evidence of Zen students who get easily caught up in their fantasies," said Roshi, while taking our pictures.

Too late, we had been set up. But now our frailty was fully exposed, I thought we might as well enjoy our euphoria.

On the way back, Roshi quietly began his Dharma talk. "While in the Seminary, you are keen to practice around the clock. The whole place is dedicated to practice, and the teacher is always available to see how you are progressing. So as long as students follow instructions and practice intently, everyone can eventually rest in the awareness of undifferentiated self and others. But once you step out of the Seminary, you are immediately confronted with the world of the separate self - the world in which self and others are often at odds, contriving, manipulating, clinging and controlling. It is extremely difficult to sustain the sense of pure oneness of self and others in that defiled milieu. Without significant spiritual strength, it is impossible. That is why you need a place like the Seminary to retreat from the secular world. Otherwise, the mind remains entangled, without any chance of liberation."

Roshi's words penetrated and calmed us straight away, leaving no trace of any delusion in our minds.

Then, he said, "A holiday house itself is not a bad idea."

I wondered why Roshi would say things almost as if to wake up the children who had just fallen asleep. There was always this inconceivable rigor underpinning his presence.

He continued, "Although you may be unaware of it, the chronic fatigue from the stress of everyday life accelerates your mental aging and pulls you down into an infinite spiral of negativity. That is why a healing milieu such as a holiday house is essential to charge your body and mind. But before pursuing such a milieu, you need to decide what the right direction for your life is. Without that sense of where you wish to go, you are bound to be drowned in the ease and pleasure of the holiday lifestyle. For an experience to be truly nurturing, you need the higher and deeper level of awareness, embracing pleasure and at the same time transcending it".

What else could we do, other than nod?

At the end, Roshi repeated, "Remember you only have the present. Live fully in the present. With one-pointed concentration just engage yourself in the present. I assure you that is the best prescription for your life."

When we returned to the Seminary, I cleaned up my room and washed the bedding, giving mind full attention to each act. In this, my third sesshin , I knew exactly what to do and moved flowingly from one thing to the next. I would say good-bye and Roshi and the other students would see me off. Everything was simple and unpretentious here.

I went to Roshi's room to say good-bye. He gave me a final Dharma talk. His way of saying goodbye. As Roshi lived the Dharma, whatever he was doing was Dharma practice. Similarly, I was not interested in anything other than the Dharma, as my sole purpose in visiting the Seminary was to search for the Dharma.

"Give all your attention to each breath. Give all your attention to a single step. Give all your attention to each moment. That is the essence of Zen practice."

POSTSCRIPT

Reflecting on my three sesshins, they brought me back in touch with the higher wisdom of the universe and the innocence of a baby. The whole experience was about my reintegration into a larger universe.

How many days had I actually spent under Roshi's guidance? The first sesshin was eleven days, the second five days, and the third four days. Only twenty-one days. Thanks to his guidance, I was able to embody the depth of Zen mind.

Many people yearn for peace of mind. Many people aspire to a higher self. I give my word. If you are enthusiastic about this path, seek the right teacher. Realization is absolutely within your reach if you commit your life to the right practice. And your enlightenment has a boundless impact on society as you illuminate the lives of people around you. To me this is a powerful reminder that I keep close to my heart; my ongoing practice has enormous bearing not just on me but also on my employees and their families.

Slowly my being is opening through practice, and I am acutely aware of the preciousness of the experience for myself. For anyone managing a business, I can emphatically say that working on purifying your own mind is the quickest and most effective way to instill unique qualities in your business. When an entrepreneur loses his or her wholesome mind, their damaging impact can be limitless, not only on employees working in the company, but that individual can also erode the wholesomeness of society.

I have seen countless numbers of competent entrepreneurs eventually disappear into oblivion. At the zenith of their business, they are proud of their super-tight schedules. But somewhere in the frantic rush of being in demand, the seed of arrogance is sewn. It grows rampantly, while their spirit remains unattended. In the end, they collapse and vanish from sight. It is a real pity that they forget to care for their inner world.

That is why I believe that entrepreneurs need a philosophy which will force them to constantly scrutinize the essential meaning of their activity beyond the trivial, and raise their self-awareness.

Entrepreneurs need to think through the long-term benefit of providing goods and services, not just for the present but for future generations. They need to cultivate fine statesmanship so they can effectively contribute to society. And entrepreneurs need to encourage consumers to develop a sense of autonomy so they can stop their desires running amok. If entrepreneurs have no philosophy, ordinary consumers may be confused about their desires and real needs. Entrepreneurs need to develop the discerning mind of educators and religious path seekers, so they can become creative designers and planners to help make this world a better place.

Doesn't it boil down to aspiring to grow into a whole person - a person who is warm, kind, caring to all, who is capable of making brave decisions and executing them, who has the strength to abide by his or her profound belief? I believe if we have this aspiration for a higher and deeper self, we have already met the teacher inherent in each of us.

And this aspiration to bring out our essence in its fullness is an absolute requisite, whether running a business, making choices in life, or raising the consciousness of employees. As long as my primary focus is on laying down the conditions for this aspiration to eventuate in a wholesome way, the rest, according to the law of the universe, will take care of itself and deliver an appropriate outcome. So, all I need to keep offering is plenty of appreciation, thoughtfulness, and trust.

As my company's president, as a tax accountant, and as a management consultant, I believe in sound business as the most important principle. The health control of any business starts from the basic vision of top management. Business, by its nature, pursues profit through legally acceptable means. But, if focused only on maximizing profit, it is nothing more than legal plundering.

However, if management upholds an inspiring vision, then business is capable of offering some of the benefits of civilization back to the community through its support of research, cultural, or educational activities.

There are two ways of looking at customers. The first merely targets them as consumers and purchasers. The second originates from the understanding that we are all part of each other living this life - the clear sense of an undivided whole and the interdependence of all things. We live together in the blessing of nature on this earth, and together we manage this world.

The vision a business upholds will inevitably result in decisive differences in management quality.

Even though cheerfulness and appreciation of each moment pervades my personal life, it is my concern for the future that impels me to strive to the utmost in my practice.

There are many signals emerging to point out that our planet earth is dying. As an entrepreneur and member of the global community, I feel genuine concern for the shadow being cast over the future of our community.

In recent years, the rising incidence of nervous breakdown is pervasive in almost every age group in Japan, and people who develop it often do not have any awareness of their pathological behavior. School children are no exception, and schools are often criticized for being ineffectual. In principle, child-rearing is the responsibility of both parents, though there are certain stages of child development that demands on enormously delicate sensibility of the mother in particular. It is critical that parents bestow plenty of attention, discipline, and gentle affection upon their children so that the children's necessary instincts and sensibility can grow in abundance.

I feel quite devastated when I think of those children who have missed the opportunity to cultivate these attributes getting married and having their own children. That is why I am anxious. I wish to remind people that the joy and hope that comes with child-rearing cannot be compared to any other activity. Child-rearing, to me, is the greatest creative art of all.

Roshi has been pointing out some of the fundamental issues of education through his unique approach, which differs greatly from that of academics. He elucidates what it means to grow into being fully human through his analysis of the essential mechanism of mental development – the conception of life, the role of DNA information accumulated throughout the process of human evolution, birth, and relationship with parents, language, and environment. He believes that most problems of education basically stem from the decline of spirituality.

If we wish to see the twenty-first century as an age of deep spirituality, we have no choice other than our own persistent practice. The effort we make will bring the clarity of mind we need to cut through to the essence of things. It is awesome to discover this spiritual strength within ourselves. But that strength is never for display, rather, it is this strength that underpins our compassion, faith, peacefulness and joy.

Lastly I offer a prayer for people to live with true peace of mind and in full possession of unshakable self-esteem.

With this prayer, my endless practice goes on.

THE RECORD OF ZEN PRACTICE: A SCIENTIST EXPERIENCE

• • •

by: Atsunobu Tomomatsu

THE RECORD
OF ZEN PRACTICE:
A SCIENTIST'S
EXPERIENCE

• • •

Atsunobu Tomomatsu

Preface

I have long been in search for the truth of life, although I have not always been aware of it. When I look back, all the joys and struggles in my life have been directed, consciously or unconsciously, toward searching for the meaning of life. During this search I happened to encounter Zen. Zen has shaken me from the core of my being to fundamentally change my mental world.

In this book I will try to describe as faithfully as possible the experience of my Zen practice under the guidance of Master Kido Inoue, the Head of Shôrinkutsu *Dôjô*. The uniqueness of this book lies in my face-to-face dialogues with the Zen Master, and the personal commentaries and comments I include concerning my experience.

There is an extensive basic literature on Zen: essays such as *Shôbôgenzô* (Treasury of the

True *Dharma* Eye, by Dôgen) sermons and biography of Zen masters like the *Rinzai-roku* [The Records of Rinzai (Chinese: Lin-chi)]; lectures on classic Zen literature such as *Hekiganshû Teishôroku* (Lecture on the *Hekiganroku*, by Tôin Iida), which were written by Zen masters or their disciples. However, Zen masters, except for a few, carefully avoided describing the actual method of Zen practice because they feared that practitioners might misunderstand it without their practical guidance. Many books about Zen have been published in English also since Daisetz Suzuki (1870-1966) introduced Zen to the West. However, there is no English-language book that describes the actual method of Zen practice in a style recording a beginner's progress. In this book I will try to describe that which I have learned from Zen master, Kido Rôshi.

The reader may be able to form some idea about what Zen and Zen practice are. I should caution the reader, however, that without actual guidance by a true Zen Master, the practitioner will never be able to practice Zen properly, even by following the Zen practice described in this book.

Some readers may recognize the implicit message of this book pointing to the unlimited roles Zen can play in various fields to liberate mankind in the 21st century, not only in philosophy, psychology, and education, but also in the natural sciences, especially brain research. The reader may also take this book as a warning of the limits on the intellect regarding our mental soundness and the limitations of Western philosophy as a basis for modern civilization.

Based upon its universality and empirical proof, Zen seems to hold a shining spot in mankind's spiritual history for these 2,500 years. I would be especially pleased if thoughtful and leading persons in their particular fields who are deeply concerned about the future of mankind would endeavor to awaken to this enlightenment unattainable through Western philosophy or modern science.

Atsunobu Tomomatsu
June 2004

Explanatory Notes

1. Japanese words are expressed in alphabet by using the Hepburn system.
2. The symbol ^ indicates a long vowel: ô and û are pronounced similarly to the "a" and "oo" in English words "law" and "pool," respectively.
3. The names of Chinese were inscribed according to Hisao Inagaki, *A Glossary of Zen Terms*, Nagatabunshôdô Co. Kyoto, 1995, in which in romanizing Chinese characters, a slightly modified Wade-Giles system is used.
4. Japanese names are inscribed in an order of the given name and then the family name although the way of inscription in Japanese is reverse order.
5. Abbreviations: c = Chinese, j = Japanese.

The First Day—Unexpected Questions

Early in the morning I left Tokyo heading west on a *shinkansen* (bullet train) and changed to a local train at the city of Mihara in Hiroshima Prefecture. I am getting closer to the *dôjô*. It was October 5, 1990.

It took no less than three months to ask Master Kido Inoue for permission to practice Zen at his *dôjô* Shôrinkutsu. Although reading a book written by him inspired me with the desire to practice Zen under his guidance, I hesitated to telephone him. I was intimidated. Still, the way he answered questions from Zen practitioners as described in the terrifying yet impressive dialogues recorded in the book moved me greatly.

Looking back at the time when I was working as a visiting research fellow with an international organization in the United States, I really couldn't get used to either work or the lifestyle there. Consequently, I nearly had a nervous breakdown. Even after returning to Japan, the symptoms did not go away. I couldn't relax, my daily life slowly giving rise to a sense of desperation.

I am a natural scientist. I believe that every human being is endowed with an intellect capable of thinking clearly by viewing matters carefully and objectively. However, I wonder if man's intellect is capable of maintaining a sound mind? "What are the limits of human intelligence?"

The more confused I became, the more I doubted the capabilities of the human intellect. I really did not know what to do with myself. It was too much for me.

The human mind is complicated and made up of many aspects. One aspect wants to escape its own mental and emotional difficulties; another aspect wants to engage in various good-willed activities; and there's a combative spirit vying to establish superiority over others. For me, all of these were in constant conflict. On top of this was the strong need to thoroughly investigate who I was. And it was this need alone that barely held me together.

I was poring over books almost at random in order to deepen my understanding of the fundamentals of the human mind. Every time I felt mentally exhausted, I would reflexively put a book in my hand.

However, the more I read, the wearier I became, and the less flexible my thinking became. Arthur Schopenhauer, a German philosopher, wrote in his book *Parerga und Paralipomena* in 1851 that picking up a book whenever you have some free time is the best method to prevent the development of your own thoughts. He goes on to say that other people's thoughts take away one's own clear judgment, bringing about one's own psychological disorders.

At that time, I did indeed seem to be suffering from this "brain ulcer" because I had almost completely lost both clarity of mind and the ability to make sound judgment.

During that time, I happened to find at the biggest bookshop in Tokyo an unusual book, *Zen Practitioners' Record: Practice Zen This Way*. It was just a book recording the experiences of several Zen practitioners, but I could somehow relate to them and became intensely fascinated by the soul-inspiring dialogues between the practitioners and the Master. The Master's recorded words that touched me the most were "This very moment is already enough."

The religion of my family is Buddhism (Shin Jôdo Shû: the New Pure Land school), but I had rarely been interested in religion of any kind. In fact, I was nearly disgusted by religion. The way religious doctrine was forced on people was just unacceptable. Not only that, blindly worshipping a God or Buddha was simply beyond my logical understanding. Despite these general feelings about religion, this book was inspiring!

I do remember, though, skimming through some Zen Buddhist literature written by Daisetz Suzuki and Kitarô Nishida in my high school days. The great ancient Zen Masters in this literature were vivid, fresh, and free of fixed ideas. Their unique character was attractive and seemed worthy of trust. I thought Zen, through unification of the mind, could be the way of overcoming the self. But I never thought that one day I myself would be practicing Zen.

In the evening when I encountered the book, having finished reading it in one sitting, I was convinced there was something exceptional about Zen. The fact that Zen was unlike other religions, which require a blind faith in a Supreme Being or God, appealed to me most. Scientific thinking and blind faith were just irreconcilable.

So I immediately decided to begin practicing Zen.

The train left Mihara, a small city overlooking the Inland Sea of Japan, and reached Tadanoumi Station about 25 minutes later. An incredibly huge steel tower with outstretching power lines identified the small country town.

A hardy-looking monk from the *dôjô* who appeared to be about 30 years old greeted me at the station with his palms joined in prayer. He drove me in a car until we reached a Buddhist temple named Shô-un-ji. In the front of the temple was a stonewall that reminded me of a Japanese castle. It looked as though it had a distinguished history.

Shôrinkutsu *Dôjô,* a small structure located behind the temple, was surrounded by bamboo groves and mountains. I was ushered to the Buddhist altar. Depending on one's perspective, the *dôjô* looked poor and simple, much like a plain, ordinary home. Void of the usual majestic-looking temple décor, it seemed in its own way very easy for a beginner to get used to the building and atmosphere.

Ten minutes later another Buddhist monk appeared. This was Kido Inoue Rôshi. He looked younger than I had expected. This was a little surprising since I had been expecting to see an older, more venerable-looking priest.

But I was impressed by his fearless appearance. Judging from his manner, I wouldn't have been one bit surprised if he had punched me there on the spot.

After exchanging a few words of introduction, I could hear footsteps in a nearby hallway.

"This is a good opportunity to meet her. I'll introduce her now." Kido Rôshi called the person out from behind the Japanese sliding doors.

A woman Zen practitioner appeared without a sound, opening the door quietly, and introduced herself. But I couldn't quite hear her name. She was kneeling down Japanese style in the hallway and spoke to me with her head lowered and palms joined together. Her neat and delicate beauty surprised me. This may well be the epitome of elegance, I thought. I had never met a person with such profound composure. I felt at a loss and imagined she represented this region's standard of refinement. After a brief introduction the woman disappeared like the wind.

Kido Rôshi then immediately started explaining about Zen practice at the *dôjô*. What he taught was just as I had expected from reading the book. Yet, his talk was so true-to-life and compelling that it somehow intensely motivated me to practice.

He explained the five essential elements of Zen practice at Shôrinkutsu *Dôjô*.

I. When sitting at the zendô (meditation hall), just give your absolute and undivided attention to breathing. Concentrate with your entire being only on breathing, Cut off the habitual mind, which causes scattered and random thinking, as soon as you notice it arising.

The state of mind where random thoughts no longer arise is called *sokkon* ("absolute present"), or *Now*. The absolute present is the world 'as it is': just as one sees, hears, and experiences without the intervention of any thought, discrimination, or consideration of any kind. The mental activities of thought, discrimination, and consideration commence being triggered by a single movement of the mind in response to activity of the sense fields.

Due to the function of successive and continuous mental activity started in this way, the real world becomes an abstraction based on words and concepts. It is a world of after-the-fact. Man lives in a relationship with his environment. This relationship initiates at the moment we receive stimuli through seeing, hearing, and feeling. This is known as the operation of the senses.

Man's distress and delusion arise from such personal opinions as hatred and ill feeling towards others, which are sparked by the working of the senses. In other words, man's distress and delusion are created by the *habitual mind* characterized by the impulsive and unnoticed linking of ideas that arise compulsively and unconsciously.

Zen is the world where all such habits have disappeared. It is the world of unrestricted activity where response to the environment is always fresh, vivid, clear of all restrictions, and free of conceptualization and discrimination. It is the world of salvation. To awaken to this world is the purpose of Zen. Through the persistent effort to preserving and maintaining the present moment, Zen practice breaks the habit of linking thoughts, which causes distress and delusion,. Many different words are used to explain the absolute present: *shikan (single-mindedness), samadhi, absorption,* the *true mind, Now,* etc. All of these point to the reality of the present moment. Strictly speaking, *single-mindedness* is "Man's free and undefiled activity just 'as it is'." It is sole activity 'as it is' at the absolute present where no thoughts intervene. *Single-minded* breathing is, for instance, the state where the breathing itself is doing the breathing, with no thoughts intervening. *Samadhi* is the condition where the mind is occupied only by the functioning senses—a state free of conception and miscellaneous thought. *Absorption* is the unified mind undivided by thoughts or notions. *True mind* is the mind without thought or with thoughtless thought. Although nuances may subtly differ, all of these point from different perspectives to the absolute present. They should be understood as the same.

II. In *zazen* ("sitting Zen") each time you breathe, turn your upper body from side to side.

Man is easily manipulated by thoughts and soon loses sight of the present moment. We can decisively and forcibly bring ourselves back to the *true mind* by turning our upper body from side to side after each breath. While sitting in the *zazen* posture it is easier to cut off random thinking by concentrating on the breathing.

However, in maintaining the same posture for a lengthy period of time a kind of constricting, local, or *polarizing* fatigue naturally arises from the strain of sitting. In brief, stiffness settles in the shoulders and back, arms and legs, etc. This *polarizing* fatigue not only makes *zazen* physically impossible, but lowers the quality of *zazen* by reducing the energy necessary to endeavor.

Consciously and tenaciously turning left and right neutralizes this harmful *polarizing* fatigue and protects against drowsiness to maintain a sound physical condition. In short, it insures sharpness of mind. The main purpose of turning left and right is to promptly discover and immediately discard random thinking, and to return to our true selves.

III. Don't unreasonably endure fatigue during *zazen*.

Zazen is neither a form of penance nor the practice of austerities. It is the "Easy Gate to the *Dharma* (Law of Buddha)." *Zazen* should not be wearisome, but should be approached in a fresh physical state with an animated spirit. To master the mind, it is absolutely necessary to preserve the present moment 'as it is'. Not a moment of negligence can be permitted. When physically or mentally tired, it is difficult to maintain the clarity of the present moment. Therefore, when fatigue arises, it is best to leave the zendô (meditation hall) and return to your room for a rest. When overly tired one's *zazen* becomes half-hearted and dull. If your legs hurt while sitting, it is all right to adjust your sitting position. Or you can do *kinhin* ("slowly and *single-mindedly* walking") in the zendô. You should not tolerate pain needlessly.

IV. Zen practice in activity should be done slowly and distinctly, in order not to lose the present moment. Decrease the speed of your movements to one-tenth their usual speed.

Zen practice can be divided into two types: practice in activity, which encompasses all the activity in one's daily life; and *zazen* (the practice of quiet sitting).

The main point of Zen practice—which is carried out in every action of our daily lives—is to preserve the present moment.

Therefore, no distinction is made between the Zen of activity and Zen of quiet sitting.

Comparatively speaking, it is generally easier to preserve the present moment during sitting Zen. At Shôrinkutsu Dôjô, until a practitioner has a firm grasp on maintaining the present moment, sitting Zen is strongly emphasized. And when doing some activity—for example: *single-minded* walking, eating, or cleaning—one's total and clear attention is given to the activity itself. This is "Zen in activity."

Each action itself is the present 'as it is'. Zen practice in activity is performing each action very slowly so that the *habitual mind* does not intervene in the present moment, or act slowly in order to recognize quickly the instant that it does. This is the purpose of slowing yourself down. When we are no longer manipulated by unperceived mechanical or unconscious behavior, we can personally experience the manifestation of what is called "*Dropping-off*," "*Satori*," or "Enlightenment." *Dropping-off* is, "the absolute condition of Perfect Freedom."

V. Whenever questions arise about your practice, immediately bring them to your Master.

In practicing Zen you may encounter new experiences, uncover new insights, and at times even go through uncertainty and anguish.

Various problems or doubts may arise preventing you from concentrating wholeheartedly on the present moment. Whenever such things arise, go to the Master to inquire about the Way. Inquiring in such a way is called *dokusan*. At Shôrinkutsu one can have *dokusan* anytime, day or night. Without *dokusan*, one's Zen practice does not steadily ripen. *Dokusan* is especially important at the outset of one's Zen practice.

Rôshi said, "If you practice in this manner, you can definitely transcend all of our concerns because each and every thing already is exactly 'as it is'. Anybody can realize this reality if his practice is correct. The reason we don't see and hear things just as they are is because unnecessary mental activity such as discriminatory thinking intervenes creating a "gap" between ourselves and the thing itself. This gap is the source of all of our concerns. It also prevents us from concentrating".

Theoretically, I may have understood this mental mechanism. However, I could not really grasp what he meant by concerns. One's own concerns are impossible to perceive by oneself, he said. I had many concerns that I couldn't eliminate, and it was after I could manage to preserve the present moment that I could perceive and begin to eliminate them one by one in my daily life.

My only interest was how to resolve this gap created by unperceived mental habits.

Rôshi explained, "The only way to do this is to utterly become the thing itself, or to become the present reality. If you really become the thing itself, the gap no longer remains and the division disappears. All unnecessary mental phenomena (all of which are generated by the gap) naturally disappear. This state of utterly being one with the thing is called *shikan* or *sokkon*. By following the five essential elements of Zen practice you can become one with your present reality 'as it is'".

Until now everything for me had just been reasoning piled upon reasoning. As I had read
Rôshi's book beforehand, I had understood his explanation of everything quite well (except for the meaning of "absolute present").

Indeed, it seemed that the present moment could only be grasped by Zen practice itself. This matter had nothing to do with intellectual understanding. In this world of the present moment words and concepts are irrelevant. This I understood by reading his book. I did not come to Shôrinkutsu Dôjô for a theoretical explanation. I came to find out what Zen actually was. And actual practice was the only way to find out.

Through Rôshi's teaching, the way to resolve my mental and spiritual torment had been revealed.

While I had thought Zen to be some incomprehensible, abstract, and mysterious religious teaching, I was astonished that Rôshi's teaching was not only concise, but also scientific and universal. I am a natural scientist. In my field, rationality, objectivity, and hard facts are essential factors in basic understanding. Based upon its universality and empirical proof, Zen has been transmitted from one Zen master to another for these 2,500 years.

Roshi said, "Zazen is empirical psychology based on actual practice, actual investigation, and actual proof.

Do you understand the true nature of this one breath?"

You must not be mistaken about this point. Scientifically speaking, breathing is the operation of the respiratory organs. But breathing is momentary function itself. In other words, breathing is only function, without any nature or character of its own. Breathing is mysterious but essential existence-without-existence, which has the direct link to our lives. It is something utterly beyond our intellectual comprehension.

Do you know why?"

This question surprised me. Had it ever been considered to investigate the matter of one's

existence by linking it directly to the present act of breathing? It is obvious that one's life depends on breathing.

But what Rôshi was saying had nothing to do with scientific understanding. Rôshi mentioned that although breathing exists as function it has no substantiality. This, Rôshi said, "Must be investigated by and within each of us".

This kind of inquiry is unknown at least in Western philosophy and probably in other religious teaching as well. It is just a matter of breathing.

Nonetheless, Rôshi asked me to investigate this most ordinary function in this way. And within this fabric, I thought I had been able to at least steal a glimpse of the incomparable profundity of Zen.

Roshi continued, "This one breath we take is the reality of the present moment. It is the phenomenal world 'as it is', totally distinct from the world of words and concepts. In other words, we ourselves are already an undeniably natural function in the present moment beyond human thought. There are none of the intellectual products woven by theoretical concepts. Theory is merely an explanation of function. But function exists only at each moment. The reality of this one breath is *shikan*. We are already in the world of *shikan* from the beginning. When this fact is clear to you, you realize there is nothing more to do. In other words, there is no self to recognize and there is nothing to realize. It is the world of the thing 'as it is'. You will see this is where the settlement lies. All notions based on intellectual and conceptual expansion drop away. You are liberated from them and get perfect freedom. This is called the Buddha's salvation, or *Dropping-off* of mind and body

What has to be done in order to clarify this?"

There was nothing to say—and no way to reply. When investigating the character of natural laws, the natural sciences deal with tangible objects in the natural world. Because natural law does deal objectively with real-world objects, it can be proven clearly through experimentation. In Zen, though, the mind is the object of investigation. You yourself must give personal evidence by clarifying your spiritual world on your own. And until you have attained absolute confidence, you have to continually and persistently investigate.

Moreover, if your attainment differs in the slightest from that of the ancient great Zen Masters, then it isn't the "real thing."

Transcending everything means everything disappears. "Selflessness" is the term used to point symbolically to that world where any concerns disappears. There is a profound realization when you've actually evidenced for yourself the objective truth of not-existing-while-existing.

This is called "Awakening" or "*Satori*." It is a personal proof of the "Great Matter" of causality. I thought the spiritual task of actually proving this to be absurdly difficult. First of all, I had to realize by myself the world of "no self to recognize and nothing to realize," the world 'as it is', and the world of *sokkon*—the state of mind where random thoughts no longer arise. Moreover, I had to give personal proof of its reality without thinking and consideration, but by using this body and mind of my own. Utilizing thought would only be confusing: however, it would be impossible to be unconscious.

I wondered if consciousness of unconsciousness could be the clue to the practice.

Then, as that thought arose, all operation of theoretical thought vanished. I had just become both the experimenter and the object of inquiry.

"It is simple. Just become one with the breath. If you become one with the breath, it will teach itself to you.

See, it's the same with the sense of taste. It's impossible to know the taste of something only through logical reasoning, because the taste itself does not exist there. If you want to know the taste of something, then you just have to eat it. The taste of the food teaches itself to you.

Do you understand? Don't try to analyze it scientifically.

Forget yourself by becoming one with the breath with all your might. One can attain the state of "as it is" just by becoming one with the breath. 'As-it-is' cannot be understood logically. It is impossible to reach the state of "as it is" just by thinking with words.

'As-it-is' must lie outside the framework of logical thinking".

Kido Rôshi's talk was very interesting. He purposely stimulated my scientific intellect using specific words and idioms. I became interested in 'as-it-isness', a state which is impossible to objectify as a scientist. I vowed to uncover the 2,500 years old mystery of Zen.

I thought to myself, "Just as Kitarô Nishida committed himself to practice Zen under the guidance of Zen Master Setsumon at Sunshin'an in Kyoto and Daisetz Suzuki knocked on the doors of Kôsen Imakita and Sô-en Shaku at Enkaku-ji temple in Kamakura, I would do the same under Master Kido

Inoue. Just as Kitarô Nishida and Daisetz Suzuki approached Zen through the study of philosophy, so would I with the assistance of the logic and experimentation of the natural sciences".

I wondered if I would reach the peaceful state of mind of 'as-it-isness', or get lost in a labyrinth of mysterious Zen concepts. My intellectual curiosity, the prerequisite quality possessed by all researchers, was stimulated all the more with the marvelous technique of the Zen Master. The only thing left to do was to verify the results through experimentation. I was eager to take on this new proposition.

The journey of this scientist looking for the state of 'as-it-isness' began like this, even though it was a pretty shaky start.

I borrowed a set of clothes from Kido Rôshi. It consisted of some outerwear with padded sleeves and a long skirt for traditional Japanese archery. I had never worn such clothing before. After putting them on, another monk escorted me to the zendô.

The zendô was a shabby sort of building that looked possibly like it had been converted from a private house. That was all that I could observe at the time, but the beautiful scenery of mountains beyond the window seemed too idyllic for Zen.

Rôshi explained to me a very simple way of doing *zazen*. "There are many ways of sitting and rules for doing zazen passed down from ancient times, but we do not rigorously observe them. You can pick them up later by yourself. If your legs are tired, you can sit cross-legged or whatever way that's comfortable for you."

He did not give me complicated instruction or other detailed rules that restrict the practitioner.

He continued, "Just throw out all thoughts of good and bad, and only concentrate on the breath. Become so close to your breathing that no thoughts have any space to arise. It's the world of things as they are. "When you are doing *single-minded* walking, just put all your attention on the soles of your feet. Just becoming one with the action and not allowing other thoughts to intervene is the secret. The entire body walking is the state of walking itself."

In the zendô he actually showed how it should be done. *Single-minded* walking is walking slowly around the zendô in sort of half-steps. There were no wasted words in his explanation, and I understood what he said very well. "It surely is the thing itself. There is nothing more to it."

The figure of this man utilizing his entire body when he walked revealed his true level of Zen attainment. He must be a very wise person.

I entered the zendô just after 3 p.m. I breathed out slowly until I had no more air left in my lungs. Then air entered the lungs naturally. I did not think unnecessary things were coming to my mind.

I felt a mysterious stillness of heart. Breathing seemed a natural function of the body.

"Does this natural stillness of breath I feel mean I am already natural?" "Does this sense of stillness belong in the category of thought?" At that time, I couldn't answer these questions.

I thought, "This is not the time for abstract cognition; it is just at a hindrance. If you explain nature using words or concepts, it only transforms this meaningful experience into some inorganic, non-living matter. Isn't such epistemology the cause of an impure mind?"

It seemed that the phenomenon of breathing as a living reality itself had nothing to do with cognition. Not only this respiratory movement of the body, but all the phenomena that take place in our bodies seems to be separate from cognition. I realized later that this discovery was very important.

At Shôrinkutsu, wooden clappers are used to call us to the dining room for meals. The

clappers rang just after 6 p.m. and everybody gathered in the dining room.

"No thoughts are arising," I timidly reported to Rôshi at dinner.

He replied, "That's impossible! You are just being carried away by thoughts, but you aren't aware of it!"

On hearing what I said he refused to believe my observations immediately. I didn't actually mean to say that no thoughts were arising. I only meant that my head wasn't full of thoughts. It was only natural that Rôshi didn't accept my observation. If I could have controlled my mind that easily, there would be no need to come to the *dôjô* to do this painful practice. Having come to practice *zazen* was a sign that a person was suffering from some psychological dilemmas and had countless incorrigible mental habits.

A fact I found out later was that Rôshi closely checks all of the practitioners from various angles. It is quite obvious to him whether or not a practitioner is at one with all his actions. In retrospect, I wasn't completely at one with mine. My mind was terribly diffused. On top of this, believing that no thoughts were arising was a telling sign that I was not really aware of myself.

This really took me by surprise later and it made me worry about, with this meager capacity for self-awareness, how much of the truth of myself I would be able to uncover. Our cognition is looser and rougher than what we think. We call this shabby cognition "intelligence" or "rationality" and believe that our self-judgment is absolute. This is totally absurd.

Rôshi said after the meal, "If you are finished eating, sit comfortably. You've been sitting in an unnatural position in the zendô for a long time, so just sit comfortably now. Whenever possible, don't senselessly try to endure pain".

I was thankful for such thoughtful and humane instruction. After every meal he would have us relax. He also thoroughly checked how our practice was going and gave us additional instruction. It was always like this at the end of meals. You could ask whatever questions you wanted and he would answer until you were satisfied. I would make the most of these opportunities. It was a very meaningful time and place for me.

When one understands one fact, the human mind seems to prompt three more questions. For Rôshi, this must have been a trying time. But for me, the practice of Zen was a "scientific experiment" putting my own mind on the table. I posed questions utterly as if the extrapolated experimental data didn't add up. I didn't want half-baked reason. If his replies were insufficient or if his talks seemed nonsensical, I was ready to run out of the *dôjô* at any time. This was not the question of the Master's competence; Zen itself was suspect to me.

"You can ask questions after you have sat Zen wholeheartedly! Don't ask stupid questions now. Just practice Zen!" Rôshi said.

This dissolved my foolish stubbornness, and I was forced to return to the zendô. Question and answer time was over. Everything was taken away from me. I felt at the same time both half-defeated and half-refreshed as I walked mindfully step-by-step toward the zendô.

I felt I wanted to rest a little more. I returned to my room around ten that evening. I couldn't fall asleep and had a restless night.

I later learned that this was due to *polarizing* fatigue. It made me realize the importance of twisting the upper body from side to side after each breath to help relieve tension and tiredness.

The Second Day—
Becoming One With My Breathing

I started doing *zazen* before seven a.m. but my back and shoulders were in pain, so I performed some stretching exercises in the zendô before resuming *zazen*.

With all my might I breathed in, and then out. Breathe in, breathe out.

I continued doing this and occasionally did "*kinhin*," slowly and *single-mindedly* walking, whenever I became tired.

At times I heard some noise, but nobody seemed to be coming into the zendô.

It was very difficult just to do the simple act of purely breathing one breath, not to mention doing it over and over again. It was not something you could do anything about since it had nothing to do with thinking. I was prone to forgetting the reason or purpose of trying to be one with each breath. And even before I would notice, my thoughts would be elsewhere. And I wouldn't even realize that I was in the middle of thinking because I was so absorbed in it. So entrenched is this habitual mind that not even effort or volition can rein it in. I would return to the present one breath only to find myself straying into thinking again. I was just repeating this recurring cycle over and over again.

There must be some sort of a powerful mechanism of the mind that habitually repeats the same pattern or action, an intellectual control mechanism that inhibits functions such as volition, resolution, and fortitude. I just had to firmly hold onto breathing to keep from straying into thought.

I asked after breakfast, "I know when breathing becomes simple and clear, thoughts don't really get involved at all. How then can I simply breathe?"

Rôshi answered, "To do it clearly and simply you just do it clearly and *simply*. "If you don't do it like that, there is no way that you can do it. There is no result without the cause."

At this point intellectual thinking jumped in. Just doing it the way you are told to do seemed stupid. Wouldn't that just be intellectual suicide?

The intellect does not really allow you to just follow instructions obediently. Like a parent trying to coerce a rebellious child into listening, the intellect requires a "why" when being told to do something.

The intellect does not accept the logic of "To do it clearly and simply you just do it clearly and simply." The intellect demands reasons. It is true that man's intelligence has brought about his own intellectual development. The intellect continues to repeat doubts and logical explanations for everything. This is both the strength of intelligence, as well as its weakness.

The intellect indulges in intellectual satisfaction but only has limited powers over human aesthetic sentiments and virtues. The reason why intelligence cannot control human action, after all, lies here. If humans rely too much on intelligence, the gap between what he says and does widens.

The contradiction of academics lies here. The intellect is not always without flaw.

Zen does not allow this kind of intellectual rebellion. Whether or not you can just follow the instructions "To do it clearly and simply, you just do it clearly and simply" is the crossroads of putting Zen into action or just searching for intellectual satisfaction. The reason why a person cannot just do a thing is due to his or her "insistence on things."

The root of restriction on human behavior lies in his "insistence on things." The essence of Zen lies where you can just simply do the thing. In the domain of "just" or "simply" one has unlimited power.

A man is free of all restraints when he just does things without miscellaneous or idle thoughts.

Rôshi's advice was to keep concentrating on the breath, without arguing the question of which comes first, the chicken or the egg. But I couldn't accept the fact that there was nothing more to it. There must be something more behind preserving and becoming a single, simple action.

Somewhere in his teaching Rôshi surely must be giving some clear and concise hidden suggestions about this.

The simple act of breathing and the cognitive operation of random thinking have an irreconcilable relationship. It is the difference between preserving this single breath, and not.

There is no choice between the two in practicing Zen.

Thoughts should be ignored right from the start. There is nothing, as Rôshi says, except putting the truth of this one breath soundly into action.

The meaning of Rôshi's words "before you start to make objections or ask questions, just do it thoroughly" was very important for me to pass the first gateway of Zen.

After dinner I was advised to eat and walk, as well as all my other actions, with more care.

Eating is such an ordinary act that you just somehow manage to do it without any particular care.

We have to make the action itself clear before we can look for the reality of the action. We must never let go of that action. You should just function naturally as a living being just doing things with your entire mind and body. That's all there is to it. But if you don't pay attention to what you are doing, you fall into the world of random thinking. And it is there where one merely experiences the shadow of true action.

This meaningless, continuous thinking process must be the habitual mind Rôshi keeps talking about. Practicing Zen means to get rid of this habitual mind. I earnestly believed this and tried very hard to prevent this phenomenon of carelessly letting go of the truth of the present moment.

From that time on, I devoutly followed his instructions and tried my best to become one with each action. There was no other way now but this. My walking speed became meticulously slow. There were times when I even made other Zen practitioners slowdown in the hall as we were walking. But to concentrate on the Zen practice I decided to ignore the inconveniences I was causing. I thought, "I can apologize after I have reached the state of "as it is'."

I left the zendô just after nine in the evening. I wasn't totally satisfied with my breathing, but I was having a less difficult time finding the present moment by paying full attention to my breathing.

The Third Day—
The Self Disappearing With Each Step

I woke up at four in the morning and went to the zendô.

In Rôshi's book I remembered reading that he examines practitioners in the afternoon of the 3rd day of their practice. I kept thinking, "I have to practice very hard today. If I don't do it today, I won't be able to answer Rôshi's questions appropriately".

I became very anxious since time was so short. But around 6 a.m. I began to feel very sleepy and went back to my room to rest. It became clear to me that this was polarizing fatigue.

'Polarizing fatigue' diminishes mental alertness to such a low level that it markedly decreases the effectiveness of one's Zen. This is why Rôshi forbids playing games of endurance.

"There is no meaning in practicing Zen in this way", he says.

I obediently and thankfully followed his kind instruction. This seemed to me a new way of teaching Zen, placing emphasis on effectiveness rather than on form. Doubtless, this would be unthinkable in traditional, monastic Zen practice.

I returned to my room remembering his kind teaching.

In a frame hanging on the wall in my room was the Chinese character *Kan*, which means 'gate' or 'barrier'.

In Zen this character indicates the gate that one must pass through to attain the Buddha Way.

I looked at this character, which was written by Giko Inoue Rôshi, Kido Rôshi's *Dharma*-grandfather in the patriarchal lineage of Shôrinkutsu Dôjô. I wondered if I could somehow pass through this gate and attain single-mindedness, too. I resolved right there that somehow I must do it.

When I woke up at 7:30 a.m., I felt well rested. I shared breakfast with the other Zen practitioners. After the meal I made myself a cup of coffee and had a couple of biscuits. Then I forced myself to go to the zendô.

As I sat, I began to feel more confident and my determination stronger. But I wasn't really improving. I would soon lose myself in thoughts within a few seconds of breathing, and I wouldn't even notice that I was being distracted. This continued for a while.

The quality of my practice must have been terribly lacking. It made me realize how weak my determination was. My resolve, willpower, and effort seemed only superficial. I was writing a check on an empty bank account. My self-confidence was seeping away. Even my self-respect and equanimity as a scientist began to crumble.

I did *zazen* alone after lunch. But I soon became so exhausted that I lay down where I was sitting (at Shôrinkutsu if nobody else is in the zendô it is permitted to lie down). I wondered if I could pass this first *Kan*. A defeated sensation gradually crept in.

For several hours I continued doing *zazen* but couldn't concentrate on my breathing at all. By now, I felt trapped and desperate. I was concentrating on breathing with all my might but still couldn't do even a single breath satisfactorily.

It's my own breathing…why do I do it so awkwardly? My desperation and fatigue only increased.

I thought to myself that if Rôshi were to come and check up on me right now I would probably feel rejuvenated.

They say that the man is endowed with the marvelous qualities of originality, independence and individuality. Moved by my own volition and resolve I had decided to practice Zen. Even so, I could not even concentrate on one single breath. I came to think that my present self was not really endowed with these inherent qualities. I could not even clarify the simple act of this one, present breath. How could something so "simple" be so difficult? Nevertheless, very occasionally there were times, just by accident almost, that I could breathe with ease. When these occasions did arise, it always amazed me. But it never lasted long.

As I watched the setting sun through a window in the zendô, I was still troubled—Is this the right way to continue doing *zazen*? I was now losing confidence somehow in the method I had been so sure of all along.

I asked myself, "What is 'conviction'?"

I didn't know.

A feeling of emptiness and meaninglessness filled my heart. Everything I had heard and believed was now proving to be of no use. It seems the human mind is structured in such a way that when it reaches its limit it becomes unstable.

Seldom in real life, do we intimately sense the gap between action and thought or the muddled state of the mind resulting from it?

The mind is usually unaware of its internal world because the self is usually carried away by externals. (After I had managed in daily life to maintain the present moment "as it is", only then I could for the first time clearly grasp such agitation in detail.)

My back and shoulders were stiff from fatigue. My legs felt like logs and wouldn't bend for sitting *zazen*. I started to do *kinhin*: I could not do anything else. When the body is under such duress, the mind becomes unstable.

Anxiety overwhelmed me. Overwhelming delusive thoughts engulfed me. I tried avoiding them by continuing to do *kinhin*.

There was nothing else I could do. I kept telling myself: "It's not impossible. I am doing it! It's good enough to take just this one step."

Almost before I was aware of it, my total attention was on the soles of my feet, desperately putting them down on the floor of the zendô as firmly as I possibly could. The thumping sound echoed in the zendô. I was struggling helplessly. If I hadn't continued endeavoring like that, I would have been engulfed in a flood of delusive thoughts.

Step...Step...Step...

The evening sunshine streaming through the window reached deep inside the zendô. It gave me a glimmer of calm and courage.

Step...step...step...

"What's the relationship between the thought 'I'm walking' and the reality of this one step? Is there really a relationship at all?"

Ideas like this passed through my head. I did not notice it at that moment, but that was the very instant I began to be aware of the existence of reality expressing itself before the conceptualization of it. It is a world where things are exactly as they are, just as Rôshi said.

We have the habit of supplementing everything we see and hear with conceptual thought. But the reality of a thing is just what it is, independent of conception and notion. I continued all the more earnestly to become one with each step.

Step...step...step...

"Huh?"

I became aware of a strange feeling. I felt as if the soles of my feet were firmly stuck to the floor.

Step...step...step...

Each step offered a growing freshness. I began to feel that the soles of my feet were by themselves firmly seizing the floor.

"Good Grief! My feet are like suction cups."

I walked around and around in the zendô doing *kinhin*, verifying this exquisite sensation I was experiencing for the first time in my life.

Step...step...step...

It came after several turns around the zendô: the fresh feeling of walking brought indescribable joy welling up throughout my body. The experience of this sensation was absolutely and supremely certain and undeniable. I stood aloof of any doubt whatsoever. Experiencing the reality of each moment 'as it is', there was no room whatsoever for words.

"Ah! This must be that what single-mindedness is!"

Intuitively I just knew this. I was sure that this real experience was a fact of reality, but I was not sure if this was what single-mindedness is. Thinking I have to clarify this, I continued walking in search of an answer to my half-doubt.

Step... step... step...

The experience of this reality did not change.

"Is this now? If this is what now is, then it is single-mindedness! Not much, but I began to feel confidence.

Then I heard the wooden clappers signaling suppertime. I wanted to get to the absolute bottom of this right now in one grand push, but I had no choice. I left for the dining room.

I said to myself, "I can't let go of this experience!"

I walked very slowly, watching each step as carefully as if I had been carrying a vessel full of water. My steps were so slow that someone passed me.

I went into the dining room hoping Rôshi would notice the unusual transformation I had undergone by the way I walked.

Unfortunately, when I walked into the dining room, Rôshi was putting something on the table and didn't look straight at me.

"Rôshi! I have understood a little about what walking is!" That was all I could say.

Suddenly he fixed his eyes on me. His eyes still scared me, but I wanted him to know my present state. I thought he should see as I demonstrate my condition 'as it is'. Just then, to my surprise, without any struggle or hesitation, I was walking in a circle in front of him. I had become that Self. While walking I got caught up in uncontrollable emotion and began to weep. I was certainly happy, but there was much more to it than just that.

The objective of the Zen practice is to settle undeniably the truth of the self, assenting to it unconditionally. The clearer the source of the self becomes, the less struggle and agony one encounters. I had not been totally liberated from all struggle and agony, but I felt tremendously relieved as struggles and agony began to diminish. The more the self-melts away, the clearer and more buoyant your heart and mind become. You become more natural and uncontrived, openhearted and genuine. My happiness at that moment stemmed from the amazement of my own personal realization of this.

Suddenly Rôshi said, "Well, why don't you sit down?"

I sat down as he said. I could not look him in the eye. I had no confidence in whether or not what I had realized was genuine and I was not certain if I could be satisfied if it had not been genuine. However, I did hope it was the real thing.

Tears trickle down my cheek.

"Do you see now? If you practice Zen in the right way, without fail you always become like this!" Rôshi was talking to one of his disciples, a heavily built fellow.

Tears did not stop; I could not look up. I took a few sheets of tissue paper from the box beside me to blow my nose.

"How many sheets of tissue paper are you going to use for a single tear? Show little more regards!" Rôshi scolded me.

Strangely enough, I didn't care. Tears were still dropping as I wept. Before I knew it, Rôshi's disciple was sobbing, too. Empathy directly felt among people striving for the same thing is a wonderful attribute of human nature.

"Let's begin the meal" Roshi said

I tried to calm down and eat, but my mind was still dancing around. The new feeling of freedom from concerns and the euphoria of finally finding this treasure generated mixed-up emotions. I was in a rather incomprehensible mental state. The meal was simple: rice, *miso* soup, croquettes, and chopped cabbage.

Just as I bit into the croquette, Rôshi demanded, "What is the taste of what you're eating?"

It was an abrupt question and for an instant the question was nothing but simple sound. But at the next moment, the significance of it surprised me. There was no way to answer by speaking.

Everything in the dôjô stopped dead, as if frozen rigid by his question. My chaotic mind instantly settled down. I became utterly calm. The instantaneous transformation was amazing. At the next moment I was simply biting and tasting the croquette quietly, deeply and slowly.

That was the taste.

I was taken by or held in its actual taste. Any further understanding was completely unnecessary. Words or concepts were not needed to emboss the reality of its taste. The taste itself was me just as I was. That was the answer.

The scientific world is a world of explanation based on words, data, and facts obtained through experimentation utilizing a skillful command of concepts and theories. If I try to explain my experience scientifically, its description would be nothing more than what follows: Food is decomposed by mastication and the digestive enzymes in saliva, which are stimulated by the sense receptors distribute on the tongue. The sense of taste is transmitted to the brain as electric signals, which perceives this sense of taste. The more we masticate the food, the more the food is broken down, and thus more potent the taste of the food becomes.

Scientific fact is truth—but mere scientific fact alone is not. If scientific facts alone are truth, then what was the emotion I so dramatically experienced? Psychologists may consider it some sort of singular illusion under unique circumstances. But, no, this is not the case. In human mental activity there is an area of emotion and sensitivity based on actual experience that is outside the area handling concepts and logic. As an example of this in the academic world, you may imagine the difference between the natural sciences and the humanities.

Did I firmly perceive or realize the existence of such an area of activity? Did I begin to become aware of the functioning senses exactly as experienced from stimuli from the outer world (the world preceding human intelligence: the world 'as it is' and the basis of the universe)?

Describing the experience in this way may arouse images of mystical experience, but this was not that kind of experience. What I perceived was just the taste of the food. The only difference between an everyday meal routinely eaten with a scattered mind and this experience was that I had forgotten myself in becoming the taste itself. This was my first experience of *Zanmai*, the state where one is totally occupied by the functioning senses alone.

Taste cannot be transmitted through words. Nor can the taste of something appear on another person's tongue by describing the taste. If this were possible, we could say that words themselves create the real world. Ultimately, there is absolutely no relationship at all between words and the actual taste of something.

No skillful and qualifying descriptions or figurative embellishments have any effect on a person who has realized the true state of things. If you try to communicate something to such a person using logic or reasoning, he will either roar at you with a thunderous cry, or he may give you a clout. This awakening was my personal discovery of an essential truth, whose influence and brilliance would be far-reaching in my future Zen practice.

Rôshi watched in silence how I peacefully chewed my food. The look on his face seemed to be saying, Very good! Well done! Mysteriously I was able to directly understand Rôshi's feelings. Here was a domain where meaningful things were communicated among people without using words, a world where perception of the self was merely a supposition. And as supposition decreased, the world became more and more transparent and clear. Apparently, a structural transformation of the mind took place, but the details of this change was still not clear to me at that time.

There was no doubt that I still dwelled in a world that utilizes words to conceptualize past experience; i.e., the world of assumption and presumption. But, thanks to Rôshi's instructions, I was able to know the world of 'now', which is born just of the present moment, the world of perception without substance or the intervention of words.

The world of 'now' must surely be the state of the universe in its true form. The universe is a real existence independent of human supposition. This was a huge discovery and a grand awakening for me. It moved me beyond words. I was already in a world, beyond science, where one actually experiences reality.

Rôshi went on, "Watch everything intently, from the movement of your chopsticks to everything about the meal. If you don't, you won't become one with the present moment. There is no other way. You only have to investigate your present activity, what you are doing right now. "If you let go of the present, you'll never attain what must become yours. You'll just be wasting your effort!

Just eat, slowly and certainly.

There is no other reality than your present activity! Things are exactly what they are!

The practice of Zen is to adhere, from beginning to end, to what you are doing. Be so utterly attached to it that there is no time or space for anything else to arise, When you utterly become your activity, the gap disappears naturally and there is nothing but the thing itself.

Whatever the circumstances, you must never let it go!

Do it slowly and clearly!"

I thought, "But I'm already the slowest eater of all!" As soon as I started thinking this, I knew it was just a random thought. I was surprised that I could now perceive clearly my state of the mind. Then I felt my mind settling down into a profound calm.

"What's happening?"

I was amazed to find I was suddenly able to recognize the slightest little movement of my hands and fingers.

"It's best we leave him alone." Rôshi said and everyone left the dining room.

Rôshi understood my state of mind and wanted me to freely practice at the highest level. I was awed by the innovative and adroit way he guides people. He made arrangements so that I could concentrate on eating without worrying about the time or other people.

With each bite I became more and more intimate with eating. I discovered that when the mind is undistracted, one finds the slow and careful act of chewing unexpectedly fascinating and the food more flavorful.

I felt the natural function of every bite as deep and significant. This feeling continued to the last. It was like the food itself made me eat. It was me; the one eating that was disappearing!

I felt like I wanted to eat a little bit more, but I put down the chopsticks onto the table unaffected by such desire. There were no obstacles, concerns, or attachments.

"What a refreshing feeling! This freedom of control over attachments is amazing!" I thought.

There was no need to stay in the dining room after I finished eating. I did not hesitate to go back immediately to the zendô to sit and continued with the breathing.

However, I still wanted Rôshi to carefully check the extent of the single-mindedness I had attained after so much effort. I think I wanted his approval as much as the invaluable experience itself. On this point, I was not completely satisfied.

I walked reluctantly towards the zendô. I sat down but the sense of dissatisfaction still remained, perhaps because the search for single-mindedness was the most important task of my visit to the dôjô and the fundamental reason why I was there. An important element to implement the mind is to utilize it for purposes that are healthy and clear. With this kind of proper consciousness of purpose alone we can avoid impure, or evil, mental functions very effectively. In contrast, when the need for self-assertion based on desire begins to operate, the mind starts running out of control. The slightest change in psychological elements can result in an unforeseen and outrageous outcome.

I was almost unable to concentrate on my breathing because the question about single-mindedness kept arising. It is no good to fall into the world of words again after the undulating mind has almost reached a point of calm. But the state of mind where questions arise one after another is really unsteady. Different from the state where many random thoughts are uncontrollably arising, this condition is difficult to manage clearly. The problem is that the doubt supplants one's concentration on the breathing. This made me wonder how in the world the mind is constructed. After sitting in the zendô for several minutes, I decided to ask Rôshi.

I went up to Rôshi's room and called him. One of his disciples was kind enough to convey my wishes to him.

Rôshi came out and took me to the dining room. We sat down face to face with the dining table between us.

I asked, "My realization, explained in words, was the sensation at my feet while walking. Is this genuine single-mindedness?"

He replied, "The sensation of your feet—or anywhere—is separate and unique. But their causal relationships are all the same"

While I was still trying to grasp what he meant, he suddenly raised his right hand up like an athlete winning a race and shouted, "What is this?"

At that moment, my right hand went up, automatically and without any doubts. That reality itself was the only answer there was. There was no other reason.

"That's right!" That was all he said.

I heard his voice, and then the sound of it was gone. I perceived and understood the fact clearly.

"Is there anything else?"

"No." As there was nothing to add, I did not say anything else.

"Watch this" He began to move his right hand from side to side about half an inch above the dining table.

I was also moving my right hand involuntarily in the same way.
Rôshi gazed at me. Then he gently stopped me gesturing with his hand. Rôshi began to move his hand again in the same way. He had utterly become one with his hand. I was utterly absorbed looking at it.

"You see this hand as if it's yours, don't you?
The eyes themselves see the hand 'as it is', and do not distinguish yours from others. Originally there is no distinction in the eye between yourself and others. The eyes themselves are not concerned at all by whatever they see.
That is the origin and nature of the self. It is completely free and liberated from everything from the beginning."

I thought so, too.
I felt that Rôshi understood things much more definitively than scientists. Rôshi had said before that Zen is the science of actual experience and actual proof. I now found this to be an obvious fact.

Rôshi went on, "The true state of the world is that all things are one. Self and other are one. Originally, everyone dwells in this 'oneness'. But people do not awaken to this reality because they have not proven it to themselves through practice. This is a great pity! This is why we have to practice."

I had nothing to say.

He continued, "Never allow a gap to arise between you and your Zen practice. Originally we are already one with things; our ears, nose, tongue, hands, legs, everything, including the mind. The problem is the gap between mind and body which prevents us from being in perfect freedom. As soon as we see something, consciousness engages and restricts the mind. This is where the 'self' arises. To remove the gap, you only need to become the activity itself. At every moment, never separate from what you are doing. Nothing exists outside of now!"

As Rôshi finished speaking he stared at me. I became purified by the strain, his warmth, and the renewed "way-seeking mind." I could see Rôshi's face clearly for the first time. There wasn't the slightest hint of malice in his look. His face was there as it was.

"Good! Now breath" Rôshi said.

I breathed in and out slowly and naturally. He seemed to be able to see right through me.

"Good, that's it. Once you breathe out completely, breathe in naturally. Continue this simple and clear natural function thoroughly as if you were a fool.
Be willing to actually die for it! It's a matter of life and death. Take a step off the top of a hundred-foot pole. Die the 'Great Death'.
Go now and continue to practice one breath."

When he said this, I realized that my previous questions and doubts had evaporated. My mind was crystal-clear. However, in no way did I want to lose that precious and genuine experience of proof. It was truly a treasure obtained through much hardship and more than anything else, I was afraid that I would lose it later.
I did not hesitate to ask, "Will someday this pure mind disappear?"

"Sure, you will lose it" His reply was quick.

It appears that our normal cognition is erected on a foundation of dualistic thinking and relativity: knowing and not knowing; attainment and non-attainment; like and dislike; right and wrong; action and inaction; perceiving and not perceiving. When we stand on this narrow plane of duality we estimate the risks of our miscalculations and even prepare for any subsequent anxiety. This kind of cognition is designed and formulated in our mental behavior.
Rôshi regards this type of cognition as the 'habitual mind', where the 'gap' arises to prevent us from seeing things as they are. This is an appropriate way of describing this pattern of cognition. If we are unaffected by duality and act on a thing 'as it is', our minds, consequently, are liberated and our agony resolved. This is the basic principle of Zen, the antithesis of duality.
Western philosophy is based on this kind of dualist thinking and conceptual thoughts. On the other hand, Oriental philosophy like, Buddhism and Taoism (the philosophy of Lao-tse and Chung-tse) are based on cognition prior to discrimination.

In contrast to any philosophy, the purpose of Zen is to remove the 'gap', i.e. it is the world beyond any concerns arising from conceptual thought. The result is called 'the True World of Reality' or 'Satori'.

I started to realize that the world of thoughts had no power at all in resolving the fundamental problem of the mind. The limitations of the world of thoughts, including philosophy and ideology, became clear to me. It was all nothing but conceptualization. Conceptual thoughts cannot resolve man's fundamental suffering. In other words, the intellect is no candidate for settling this matter of the Self.

Thus, Zazen practice removes the origin of our suffering, which is called the 'gap'.

Rôshi's words came to mind, "You lose what you have gained. What has been gained can only be lost. Throw away absolutely everything and utterly become the one breath itself.

If you get rid of anything and everything, you'll have nothing to lose. At any point in time, and at any place, things are exactly what they are. When everything disappears, everything becomes the Self 'as it is'. There is nothing else but that. You should know this well.

This is the world of Zen"

Philosophy, ideology, and science are useless here. Zen is actual experience, not a philosophy or ideology. Zen is to realize the 'Absolute World'; things as they are, preceding cognition and to dwell in that universal world. No theory can account for the world of 'as it is' which is nothing and everything at the same time.

But still acknowledging this, I had the growing desire to understand intellectually what Zen was, and to theorize and articulate it. Being a researcher, I felt that was my mission.

Intellectual satisfaction based on intellectual interpretation is a very dangerous pit hole that Zen practice beginners can fall into. One needs to be aware that theorization about Zen only causes serious problems for those who theorize and those who read those theories. Writing or reading about Zen can significantly disturb one's practice, often leading to such things as fault findings and self-justification. Thus, practice is imperative under a guidance of a true Zen Master.

Zen is the act of letting go of everything you have gained; learning is the act of holding on to what you have gained. Learning makes people clever; Zen makes people fools. However, we must know that this kind of foolishness has great power and authority. No theory is required to become a fool.

The clever people seek for theories, which turn out to be additional delusion.

Rôshi said to me, "The world of the intellect, after all, differs from the world of the body. Notions and concepts are woven into words by means of logic. There is no time or space in words. The world of thoughts is inorganic and superficial.

But our bodies are an actual objective existence. This body is reality and existence at this moment. In other words, each of our bodies is the existence of pure function.

Life is the active relationship with the outer world carried out through the functioning body. Life is just these functions taking place in our body. The persons who individually and purely experience and savor each moment like this with undivided attention are called the ancient great Zen Masters".

He continued, "Regardless of being known or unknown, everyone is using the *Dharma* (our true Reality) perfectly from morning till night. Moreover, no trace remains; everything finishes of itself at each point in time and at each place. This is the work of emptiness, the function of nothingness; it is, in other words, salvation. Making this matter clear is called 'Satori' The purpose of Zen practice is to attain 'Satori'. It means our mind working according to reality. According to reality means no separation or gap. It is the thing 'as it is'. To function according to reality means to become one with just this, your present condition. If you try to become the thing itself or the activity itself, it will only double your delusion. The only thing to do is to devote yourself exclusively to the activity. For as long as you have not clarified this, it will be painful for you because you will not properly deal with it.

At times like that, just start again from one breath.

Breathe out and breathe in. It demands great zeal and close attention to prevent yourself from dropping into scattered thinking. It is not until you have completely exhausted every means that the 'self' drops off ".

He then questioned me, "Could you possibly permit yourself now to separate from the present moment? Could you let your breath at the present moment get away? Zen practice is to throw away everything. But you try to accept, preserve, and protect a lot of junk. Don't you understand?

His look became more intense as he said, "This is the very cause of delusion. You're an idiot! That is why your practice does not work out to your satisfaction! Real Zen practice starts from now!"

"The light and hope you have attained can grow only when you throw them away each moment! With great perseverance you have reached this stage, so try hard to continue your practice with great care!"

As he finished his words, I felt the need to practice more. As I was about to stand to go to the zendô, Rôshi who was staring at me, slapped hard a table. Bang!

At the same time he shouted: "What is this?"

With a little hesitation I also slapped the table.

"You must have been thinking. For a second you had lost yourself in thought.Why do you still carry such a big 'gap' in your practice?

That kind of Zen practice is no good!

In now, just 'as it is', there is no room for such a gap!

What are you waiting for?" He finally asked

" "

As soon as I started to think, I fell into confusion.

"Go to the zendô. Now! Do not ask me stupid questions anymore!" He scolded me loudly.

If I had been within his reach, he would have slapped me for sure. I pressed my palms together in *gasshô* and headed for the zendô.

The feeling of ecstasy had disappeared completely. My mind continued to settle down to reach a profound tranquility that I had never experienced before.

I realized how great Rôshi was.

I assumed that perhaps I had gone through the gate that Zen practitioners must pass through. I felt happy that Rôshi confirmed as a definite experience the small clue I had uncovered.

Unexpectedly, merely the sensation on the soles of my feet had been the gateway to such a wonderful world. This was totally unexpected, and unmistaken. Finding the entrance to single-mindedness, together with Rôshi's advice and encouragement, gave me an unwavering confidence in my Zen practice.

While I was walking I could not stop thinking, "Perhaps the difficulty and painful struggling in my Zen practice is over now."

Then, realizing the pitfalls of such devilish thoughts, again and again I admonished myself, "Beware of such heretical demons!"

When I opened the back door of the main building and began walking on the duct boards leading to the zendô, my single-minded walking was in disarray because of these thoughts. I keenly realized how easily the mind becomes unsettled, and how immature my own practice really was.

I had been in the zendô for a while when the hardy-looking disciple of Rôshi's named Sogen walked in. He wore the black, formal robes of a monk. Bowing and sitting in the traditional manner of a monk, he began doing *zazen*. The monk swung his body fully left and right, and breathed out deeply.

I started to enter to the single-mindedness as well by hearing breathing. It was the same situation as when I realized that I had become Rôshi's hand when seeing his hand move left and right slowly over the table.

It felt rather odd since it was not an intellectual recognition of the disciple's actions. My entire body felt and responded to it. For sure, we are something other than just intellectual beings.

Ours is an existence of more straightforward and distinct processes. And we would best regard as delusion any failure to recognize this unquestionable fact.

The Fourth Day—
Listening To The Master Is Crucial

In the evening I was permitted to take a bath for the first time in four days. The hot water felt great. It felt like I was really alive for the first time. I took the bath in a simple and unconcerned manner, and was out before I knew it.

A modest party at supper was held for me at 8 pm that evening. It was a midterm observance for my efforts thus far. It was nice having the party. I like to drink, and I drank quite a bit—as much as I wanted—since I was exhausted from the practice. I felt like I could have drunk endlessly. It was remarkable that I did not feel drunk. It seemed like some vast and perfectly clear spiritual power was at work within me.

I listened to Rôshi speaking about his views on the world. He spoke a lot.

Listened, I *just* listened.

But when I had something to say, I also talked. Up until that time, I only asked questions.

I spoke about the idea of establishing a think tank based on Oriental thoughts for solving the world's problems. Rôshi, kindly listened showing some interest.

I wanted to argue that scientists, whose commodity is their intellect, are also in great need.

But I could not confidently say it because I knew from personal experience that the scientific intellect presents, in some cases, contradictions when aligned with human nature. Intelligence and humaneness must dwell as one in the personality. The scientific intellect alone is a handicap.

I read the *Rinzai-roku* (c: *Lin-chi-lu*) when I was a high school student. The book refers to the following story. A monk, Head Monk Ting, Ting Shang-tso, asked Zen Master Rinzai (c: Lin-chi) about the fundamental principle of Buddhism and got slapped. The monk was then scolded by another monk, who was standing near the Master Rinzai, saying, "Why don't you bow to the Master?" So the monk bowed. At this moment he attained Great Enlightenment.

I remember that I could not understand why the monk became enlightened in that situation. It was puzzling. My failure to interpret this anecdote might have encouraged me to practice Zen.

I related this little episode to Rôshi. And he said, "You were a bit precocious for reading the *Rinzai-roku* in your high school days. The monk forgot himself when he was slapped. In other words, the 'gap' disappeared. At the moment he was scolded, he realized there was nothing, and that everything was one. This is an interesting episode of sudden Enlightenment."

I recall that I read many books like that in those days. However, I realize now that I misunderstood what they meant.

I was the only one who slammed his heels on the floor so loudly while single-minded walking. I was perhaps also the only one who asked so many questions.

Asking so many questions is inherent to a scientist. A scientist pursues the question until an answer is found. When understood, then there is no need for further questions.

During the period of a young child's intellectual growth it will develop intellectual interests and their world of cognition when, we, adults completely answer their questions one by one. In this way, children acquire the habit of thinking through things. The ability of being able to make an appropriate question is clearly a evidence of an intellect working with a precise awareness of the issues. Childhood inquisitiveness helps develop a scientific mind, the initiative for problem solving, and a healthy independence. A Zen practitioner asks questions as a child would. Questioning is the key to Zen practice. A Zen practitioner improves his or her level of practice by questioning. When a Zen master answers fully, we naturally become more eager in our pursuit of the Way.

The Fifth Day—
The Vital Point Of
Returning To The Present Moment

I woke up at 4:30 a.m.

I tried to concentrate on the one breath, but it was difficult. Thoughts poured out ceaselessly. Most of these thoughts were about what I was not able to fully express the night before at supper. I thought I spoke without reservation, but I must have left something unsaid. This must be "the hell" that a beginner suffers from and must pass through.

Rôshi had already warned me the night before of what I would go through the following day. "Tomorrow you will be scattered and unable to concentrate and you will not be able to return to the present moment until around midday. Do you know why?

All of this talk you are engaging in means that the habitual mind, which used to have a grip on you, has revived.

Originally, at the present moment nothing arises: it is a world of no before-and-after, no habits, of nothing at all. You must penetrate thoroughly the present moment to get rid of the gap. Your clouded mind has just started to clear up, but it still stirs up easily. You've just started to get the feel of what the present moment is.

Because the habits of the habitual mind are still alive, as soon as the lid to the intellect is opened, immediately all sorts of devilish mental phenomena start up."

Rôshi explained that last night's party at supper was also held to break down the unified state of the mind. "When someone returns again to the regular world, he or she will soon lose the unified mind. Therefore it is essential to grasp the vital point of immediately returning to the present moment."

As I sat doing *zazen*, I realized how scattered my mind had become. Our minds are as unsettled as grass waving in the wind. The cause for this instability is that the mind's reaction to circumstance is not unified, unnecessary, and instantaneous. When the internal conditions that create such attributes as conviction, will, and resolve breakdown, then these qualities deteriorate and pale to the point where we lose in an instant the ability to continue our focus on the matter at hand. Consequently, even when we are consciously engaged in conceptual or intellectual processes, there is no guarantee the mind will be unruffled. Perhaps the only way to secure peace of mind fundamentally, and at every moment, is through proper Zen practice as taught at Shôrinkutsu Dôjô.

Because I could not concentrate on my breathing, I decided to slip into my futon again and slept until seven o'clock a.m. Then I got up to sit *zazen*. I was immediately able to unify my mind and fix it on a single point. This was also an unexplainable reality. Once again, I understood my fatigue, the relief from fatigue, and the tremendous power of one single breath. This was the result of the toil and labor I had gone through at the dôjô and I was thankful for my efforts. I had been worried that I would not be able to return to single-mindedness. But this realm into which I had put my faith proved to illuminate the way.

It is impossible for a beginner to understand the state of mind of the practitioners who is several steps ahead. The beginner cannot even begin to know what stage a senior practitioner is in or what sort of Zen practice he or she is doing.

Shôrinkutsu Dôjô's Principles of Conduct state, "While in the Dôjô, never think right and wrong; *simply* act according to the *Dharma* at each moment."

The primary objective of these Principles is to preserve one's single-mindedness no matter what the situation may be. Whether you are taking a rest in your room, drinking coffee (or even having a drink), walking, cleaning, taking a bath, or going to the toilet—in other words, at any time and any place and in any circumstances—you must try to maintain your grasp on the present moment continuously and preciously paying extremely careful attention to every single movement you make. This requires more effort and persistence than one could imagine. And a beginner isn't yet able to see the do-or-die efforts made by senior practitioners, even in their everyday actions, to preserve this single-mindedness. The great Zen Master Dôgen said, "To study the *Dharma* is to study the Self."

Inoue Rôshi clarified this in a refreshing manner saying that Dôgen's words mean not to lose oneself even for a second."

In comparison to any other Zen dôjô, Shôrinkutsu may seem at first glance to have rather lenient rules. Except for *zazen* and sutra recitation scheduled in the morning, your time is free to do whatever you wish. But Rôshi and the older practitioners can tell in a moment if a beginner has strayed from single-mindedness. They can notice this even from a single sound someone makes.

I can say without a doubt that this dôjô is the strictest in Japan. When comparing Shôrinkutsu with other traditional dôjô-s, it is obvious that traditional dôjô-s make emphasis on customs and forms rather than on the essentials of *zazen*. It is not difficult to say which is truly stricter.

The reason why Shôrinkutsu has carried on since its founding by Master Tôin Iida Rôshi is due, without a doubt, to the Dôjô's Principles of Conduct.

How to *just* sit when sitting, how to *just* eat when eating, how to *just* see when seeing, how to *just* sleep when sleeping, and how to keep focused on the present moment are all explained in the five guidelines of the Principles of Conduct.

But, even while at the dôjô, one's Zen practice at times may lose its vitality and start thinking in terms of good-and-bad and right-and-wrong. One can begin to wonder about others' Zen practice and may start judging and critiquing about their efforts and progress. When judging others like this means, undoubtedly, that one has wavered the 'Way'. Perhaps I should rather say that when your resolve has weakened you start thinking about others around you. Zen practitioners must take great care about this. It was only after repeatedly falling into such mistakes that I was able to avoid this pitfall myself.

There was a monk whom I had met several times at Shôrinkutsu who often would criticize others. The comments he made about others were superficial and biased, and he seemed unable to see his own character flaws. It is frightening when a Zen practitioner loses the ability to follow the teaching and true practice. He finally began saying things like, "This is not a Zen dôjô. It's like a hospice."

Why did he seem so blind?

Probably, he lacked the nature or disposition to follow the teaching at Shôrinkutsu. Someone who does not make the needed effort to thoroughly investigate and clarify the Self cannot be called a Zen Practitioner. It would be unthinkable for anyone who is wholeheartedly absorbed in his practice to judge others. While practicing Zen and judging whether other people are right or wrong means that your practice is for the sake of your own self-righteous interests. You cannot be called a true Zen practitioner.

Those who only make immature and superficial judgments and do not seek the 'True Self' are not welcome at Shôrinkutsu. Even if there were such Zen practitioners in your midst, you should not judge raising views of good-and-bad or right-and-wrong. This is what distinguishes the capacity of a true Zen practitioner.

The Sixth Day—Become A Real Human Being

I finished cleaning the garden around 10 o'clock in the morning. Then I stepped out for a walk to Tadanoumi, the little town where the dôjô is located. It was my first visit to the town since I arrived to the dôjô. Everything was fresh and alive. They say that it only takes about 30 minutes in town for a practitioner to lose his grasp on the present moment. I was afraid of this at the beginning but gradually I gained courage. I could keep the present moment without random thoughts interfering. I was able to *just* see and *just* hear as I walked around the town.

After tea time at the dôjô I climbed up the mountain behind. Beyond the scattered gravestones in the graveyard, the Inland Sea of Japan spreads out. It was remarkably beautiful but it was still just an experience within the sense of my sight. No thoughts crept into the scenery. The pine forest enclosing the view looked like a large, Japanese folding screen. It was infinitely refreshing.

Right at that moment, I let out a deep groan. My insides shook. Before me, stretched the world independent of words! Words would not form in my head, as hard as I tried. No words whatsoever connected to anything. I saw the world—the natural, normal, real world itself–absolutely free of words. There was just the world of reality and myself. It was nature itself.

"Clear mirror and still water!" [This saying means, seeing nature 'as it is'.]

It became clear to me that mountains, rivers, grass, and trees—all have the Buddha-nature.

My hot belly trembled all the more as tears trickled down my cheeks.

"In my entire life I have never been so deeply moved."

I was moved by overflowing emotion from the bottom of my heart and continued to shed tears of sincere gratitude to Nature itself and to Rôshi for this unforgettable experience. In the afternoon I went to a coffee shop in town. I deliberately wanted to look at nude magazines, which these shops often made available for their guests. At first I was unmoved, but gradually words started forming in my head little by little. Words like "Oh" or "Good Grief!" began to emerge. I was experimenting: under what circumstances and in what manner would my mind become confused?

I knew that tempering–or "kneading"–single-mindedness is not enough when one finds the mind confused. One learns how to really "knead" the mind by experiencing the harshness of the regular world. My way of Zen practice has included an endless number of such psychological experiments.

Rôshi gave a talk that evening and afterwards I asked Rôshi about the biggest question in my life: What should my goals be?

He kindly replied, "When planning your future, the most important thing is to choose something you like. Do not set goals that are beyond your capabilities because trying to achieve them will burn you out. Learn how to behave within the social structure—consider your relationships in both the vertical and horizontal makeup of the structure. Anyone who cannot do this cannot be considered an adult. In a social organization, one develops abilities beneficial to the organization but not his true individual talents since it is not one's own world of individuality".

He continued, "Be willing to wholeheartedly invest your brain power, money, and passion in a positive and sound objective. Rise above loss-and-gain, duty, and obligation; just follow your convictions. A sense of purpose is one of life's fundamental requisites. Hold on to them at all times. In order to achieve your goals, do not lose the present moment. Results are attained naturally if certain conditions have been achieved. Accumulate the causes that affect the desired result. Everything changes. Just as bad things pass so does good things; value the present moment. Reflecting on the past is good, but don't hang on to the past."

"Don't forget the fact that you will die someday. Credibility, virtue, honesty, and sincerity are your best friends, along with the willingness to make an effort. After you have done your best, the result is in the hands of the working of cause-and-effect. It is useless to judge the result as right or wrong. A heart that feels gratitude and thanks is the most beautiful and valuable quality of man's character. Goodness or wholesomeness that has not been realized by resolving the problem of the *gap* is easily shattered by slander and groundless rumors, simply because it is not genuine goodness.

Behind ordinary and primitive love are concealed the frightening and violent feelings of hatred, jealousy, and anger, that at times, can develop into the desire to kill. This arises from the power of life and the instinct to survive."

Rôshi's talk gave me plenty to think about.
As my life's goal, I wanted to attain the things he talked about.

When I was thinking about my future, Rôshi suddenly said, as if he had seen through me,
"If you have the kind of character that would not let you to be satisfied with small achievements, then you may as well die the Great Death."

"Me? Do I take this all the way to the end?"
What he said surprised me at first, but inside I was not really surprised. Perhaps Zen was the very thing I had long been searching for. I had taken Zen to be a means in my life, but he was saying to make it the goal. Anyway, this did seem a bit extreme!

That day, when I had that unforgettable experience while looking at the sea, made my trust in Zen unshakable.

My favorite things had been scholarly accumulation, searching for the truth, appreciation of the arts, and self-training. They were really very ordinary pursuits. But I was not fully satisfied by them. Outside of Zen, there was nothing that would allow me to pursue them tirelessly. Zen is wonderful because it is complete and lacks nothing.

"As your Zen practice progresses, you will be able to see and understand things much more clearly. You attain a universal point of view. You attain an all-encompassing and profound foresight into life, along with a deep appreciation for and keen interest in it". As Rôshi said this to me I realize that a universal point of view and profound foresight are indispensable qualities for living one's life.

"After you return to regular life, you should sit every day in the morning and evening. The regular world becomes your dôjô. At work, just do your job objectively, and without the 'gap' between you and the thing itself". In your social life, just continue to 'knead' the present moment. You will then be able to work effectively without experiencing stress. Think of your daily life as religious practice, and make good use of everything because it is Zen practice."

Rôshi's instruction was an easy-to-understand, practical handbook for daily life.

"Social life is filled with manifold objectives. It is a realm where one must respond to them seeking specific results. To do this, we use our body and mind in order to affect the desired result. This is what social life is.

We are endowed with the six sense organs: eyes, ears, nose, tongue, body, and mind. These correspondingly function with the six objects: shape, sound, odor, taste, sensation, and mental phenomenon. The mind works according to natural law responding to time and events. It functions according to circumstances, or conditions. When these circumstances pass or elapse, no trace of them remains anywhere. Delusion exists nowhere. Even Enlightenment, or good-and-evil, arises in response to time and circumstances then vanishes without any trace. It is said that delusion and Enlightenment are one, but no such thing as delusion or enlightenment can be found in the functioning senses themselves. It doesn't seem that in the regular world delusion could be identical with Enlightenment. Delusion, which is caused by the gap between you and the thing itself, creates problems because one thinks in terms of before-and-after. Enlightenment is 'Dropping-off' because there is no gap between things like front and back, or before and after.

You should understand that even the slightest gap produces a broad deviation.

We produce results, ultimately, by using our minds and our bodies. Our relationship with the outside world is within those realms only. The functioning of our minds and bodies themselves are causality 'as it is'. It is the condition of the present moment, Now. Now is Now. But not remaining in Now is the true Now. Zen practice is to realize this from the bottom of your heart and soul. There is nothing in the world to become attached to. The Way is to simply do things." Rôshi, after saying this, pause for a moment.

He asked me, "But you do understand these things? Don't you?"

Looking at me, Rôshi carried on, "Whatever you see, hear, write, lift, or put down, whenever you sit, stand, or walk—everything you do—capture that moment in minutest detail. And when it is finished, be done with it. This is the vital point in simply doing the thing itself. That is all there is to our lives. Our lives are made up of our present actions, one at a time. The crux lies in whether or not we are simply doing things, or not. Life depends on whether or not our actions are in accordance with phenomenal reality. In other words, are we simply doing things, or not?

This sweeping statement points to the world of oneness where we become the thing itself. An ancient great Zen Master said, 'The Way is independent of knowing or not-knowing.' This is the natural world prior to perception. The only thing to do is to stop evaluating and simply act in response to what happens each moment. Because there is no 'self' we assimilate with reality and are filled with a sense of truly living in profound satisfaction. When you find that there is really nothing you must do, you experience with your entire being the serene self that exists simply and in the present moment. You experience everything with your entire being. And because you experience the thing 'as it is', there is no lack or excess. This is called the 'Way' or 'Zanmai'.

Zen practice is to simply act according to what happens in the moment".

This talk contained his most important instruction. It was a concise explanation of our mental attitude toward practicing Zen in our daily lives.

"An elephant does not stroll along a rabbit trail. Do not congratulate yourself for little achievements!". Rôshi's unique way of scolding someone while encouraging them at the same time was wonderful.

I wanted to say something to him but couldn't find the words.

"The effort to preserve single-mindedness and leave behind random thinking is called the Way."

How much these words moved me! I knew the word 'Way' but I never knew how straightforward the word was.

"Become a man that saves the world. Mankind has nowhere to go but to ruin, poisoned by the civilizations that man himself has created with his intellect. Today, where man's ego has grown excessively large, it is urgent to restructure the family and society to foster human virtues and independence in their true sense.

Take a look at most of the families today. Fathers and mothers are not fulfilling their roles as parents. Consequently, manners and morals are not fostered in the growing family. The result will be the development of a mental makeup lacking in courtesy and a sense of responsibility.

Character traits of thoughtfulness and consideration for other people or the larger good have been forfeited to self-centeredness and personal pursuits conveniently labeled in the name of 'freedom' or 'independence.' They are without principle, order, or discipline, and lack any reason for existence. They live merely like human animals. They have no views on life, the nation, or the world. Their only view of life is based on egotism and complaining. They have no healthy ideals or dreams since they have not developed the faculties of systemic planning and construction. They have been deprived of the essential elements of natural growth and development; accordingly, they do not know what they want to do or what they have to do. Under such circumstances, society falls into ruin.

This is a terrible situation!

We need true leaders now, leaders who have realized the true Self.

"Don't you think so? If you don't, you could not be human!

It is up to yourself to begin! Will you? Or won't you?"

His talk influenced me greatly. He was saying to be a True man first, then a scientist or researcher.

I was concerned about how individual happiness achieved by Zen practice was conveyed to others. This was very important and I was happy to hear that as one becomes a whole person, he or she gains the ability to give back something valuable to society.

No one could say "no" when asked, "Will you, or won't you?" But if you answer "yes," however, it only sounds like lip service.

There could be no way to convince Rôshi other than by showing him actual proof.

When that happens, his heartfelt blessings will be with you, I am sure.

It is said that to really see a Zen practitioner's true form just look at his daily life. One can surmise his or her *kyôgai* from their everyday actions. *Kyôgai* is the mind's eye that sees through human nature and has the virtuous power to influence people; i.e., one's sphere of understanding of human nature and compassion toward other human beings.

I could hardly assess Rôshi's *kyôgai*. There is warmth in his eyes and kindness in his words. Sometimes he roars *Katsu!* Sometimes he drinks. Sometimes he sings. His teaching ranges from how to practice Zen to the essence of education, the philosophy of art, and the affairs of politics. The depth of his single-mindedness is clear when he drinks tea or types on the keyboard of his computer. There are countless things he has said that have left a deep impact on me.

The Seventh Day—
A Once In A Lifetime Encounter

At noon I practiced single-minded walking and breathing in the graveyard behind the dôjô. I was absorbed in doing a single deep breath without any thoughts. This unquestionable stillness, I thought, was like the immovable mind. Although I had heard the term before, it was the first time I really realized what the power of 'Absorption' was. How firmly my mind has stabilized! My mind suddenly realized and accepted the Confucian teaching, "To have heard the Way in the morning, it is all right to die in the evening."

In the afternoon I went into town and happened to stop in a small noodle restaurant. An old woman, about my mother's age, started talking to me. She talked about her poverty and the great difficulties she encountered right after the Second World War. By coincidence, she mentioned the wife of Ryûzan Inoue Rôshi, the elder brother of Kido Rôshi, and related how Ryûzan Rôshi's wife used to share food with her at the time of the great food shortage after the war. I was moved to tears by her story. When I left the restaurant I joined my hands in prayer in gratitude for her sincerity. I did not think I would meet her again.

"This must be the spirit of tea ceremony," I thought, "One encounter, once in a lifetime!" The essence of Zen is supposed to be difficult to attain, but I was able to discover it naturally and directly. I never expected before I came here that my mind and heart would be transformed in such a short time.

I shed tears of gratitude to Rôshi on my way back to the dôjô. At the same time, the resolve to die the Great Death became firm.

I told Rôshi of the various changes my mind had undergone an he replied me, "When we practice Zen, impurities in our mind drop off, and our thoughts gradually become true."

It is quite a wonderful phenomenon when modesty, gentleness, thankfulness, and kindness manifest in my attitude toward others as one's mind and heart, without being aware of it; becomes purified. It was remarkable that just this one breath had reordered the mental environment for this transformation, in spite of the fact that I had never practiced Zen for such a purpose. This is a world that psychologists and educators do not know about nor could ever dream of. Zen is indeed a miraculous world.

The Eighth day—
Give Yourself Up To The Work

During the morning *zazen* I tried to count how many thoughts would arise in my mind. When a single thought appeared, I counted it as one. If I said to myself, "A thought just appeared," I also counted that and the count doubled. However, the count itself—one, two, three—I did not count as thoughts. I estimated the thought count at 54 in 30 minutes. A single thought occurred once every 33 seconds. I have the disposition of a natural scientist; I wanted objective data to determine if my random thinking occurred too often or not. I was extremely earnest.

I reported my finding to Rôshi. He said I had too many thoughts, and then scolded me, "Don't do such foolish things, you poor intellectual!"

What Rôshi seemed concerned about was that I was scientifically analyzing Zen from the

relationship between random thinking and time. Analyzing Zen inevitably harms the practitioner.

First of all, analyzing one's Zen practice is far different from single-mindedness because analyzing erects both a self-practicing Zen and a self-analyzing it. This kind of Zen practice is dualistic. It is impossible to attain salvation through dualistic thinking. The suffering of mankind is brought about by creating numerous selves in such a way. Zen is the means to prevent such divisions from occurring. In Zen practice one becomes the thing or action itself, be it eating, walking, speaking, etc.

The second reason—one that is especially applicable to a scientist— is that humans become attached to the cognizant world which has been created via one's thinking activity. Zen practice is void of any intellectual knowledge, comprehension or discrimination. It is the effort to maintain single-mindedness and is the world of non-attachment to the cognizant world erected from past experience.

Third, if one starts to analyze single-mindedness, it is no longer single-mindedness. An analysis of single-mindedness might be considered to be scientific study, but it is not Zen practice.

It may be possible to make Zen an object of scientific analysis. However, scientific analysis could never expand one's *kyôgai*. After that time, I often found myself at a crossroads between continuing to practice Zen and analyzing it. There is no doubt now that the spirit of an experimental scientist, however, has subsequently been the driving force in my Zen practice.

"Today forget your breathing, and let your breathing breathe as it does. Ignore arising thoughts in your mind." At the end of breakfast, Rôshi chased me into the zendô with these words.

His instruction seemed very difficult to put into practice, especially for a beginner like me. "Ignoring arising thoughts and emotions without dealing with them," seems easy at first, but it is actually quite difficult. Mental phenomena—thoughts, concepts, emotions, etc.—arise instantaneously, without relation to time or place. This also happens, of course, while doing *zazen*. Once a single movement arises in our minds, we tend to associate it with the thought arising the next moment.

And so we start to think in continuously increasing thoughts like this.

An ordinary person is not able to recognize the moment that a single movement of the mind occurs or finishes. This is because most people think in a continuous stream of thoughts and have never clarified for themselves the condition of the mind without arising thoughts where before and after are cutoff. But by practicing *zazen* we can recognize the state of "before-and-after cut off," and we can maintain it. We are then capable of ignoring any arising thoughts in our mind.

What is the difference between an ordinary man and a man who practices Zen? The ordinary person does not know the state of things as they are. He or she is easily confused and captivated by thoughts and emotions. But by Zen practice one attains or realizes the absolute present moment Now. Having attained this, you can cut off any arising thoughts consciously, and maintain the present moment without any arising thoughts.

Only the person who has experienced the absolute present moment can ignore arising thoughts, and leave them alone without dealing with them. The most effective way of doing Zen practice is not by trying to cut thoughts off, but by ignoring them without dealing with them at all.

This is the shortest path to Enlightenment, but it is impossible for a beginning practitioner to do. The beginner only loses his way when following this method and spends most of his time in confusion and doubt.

Other Zen masters, whom I have met, splendidly explained the truth of Buddhism or the *Dharma*, but I was not satisfied with their general guidance because they did not understand my mental condition sufficiently and they failed to guide me properly according to my level of practice. They seemed to be lacking in practical analysis and understanding of humanity.

But Kido Rôshi was able to 'scratch where the itch is.'

The aim of Kido Rôshi's initial instructions for Zen practice is, above all else, to quickly and firmly gain the ability to ignore arising thoughts. Our cognition is based on the delusion of attachment. Accordingly, in order to precisely master the practice of Zen, step-by-step instruction according to one's level of understanding is essential. Originally there are no steps in the *Dharma*, but guidance for a practitioner without consideration of his or her personality would result in their bewilderment. Ignoring arising thoughts is at the highest level of Zen practice. This is what single-mindedness is. But if this kind of practice is given to the practitioner who isn't ready for such practice, it would probably lead them into bewilderment. Medicine, if improperly administered, can become poison. If this had been given to me in the beginning stage of my practice, I would have surely lost my way.

Nowadays we have easy access to the records of the ancient great Zen Masters such as the *Shôbôgenzô*, the *Mumonkan*, and the *Hekiganroku*. But we can hardly understand them; much less apply them to our Zen practice. As outstanding and excellent these records may be, the question of understanding them arises in the level of one's Zen practice. A Zen Master named Daie of ancient China burned the *Hekiganroku* because he was afraid that it would confuse Zen practitioners. I think he did this because of his great mercy and passion for all living beings.

The teaching, the records of ancient Zen Masters, or even Zen Masters themselves can become either poison or medicine for a Zen practitioner, if dispensed inappropriately. Although we rely on them for guidance, we have to take care not to become attached to nor become dependent upon them. Zen dislikes the practice of blind obedience. We believe in the teaching; but at the same time, we must not become attached to it. An assimilation of the subtle contradiction between these two is the essence of Zen practice. There are many people who cannot think without an established framework. I doubt these people could understand the paradoxical framework of Zen. Therefore, a Zen teacher must be a true master who has really experienced Enlightenment and personally knows the way to salvation. Only a true master of the Way can lead others in such a way that they don't become attached to the teaching.

My time was spent simply as it naturally passed. I could finally practice single-minded sitting. "Ignore arising thoughts" means, do nothing.

Kido Rôshi had said before that this 'methodless-method' is the true method of Zen practice. I could really understand what he meant (but I never expected at that time that I would still be making on-going, extreme efforts for a long time to come in order to master this methodless-method).

Rôshi gave a *Dharma* talk at afternoon teatime. The talk was about the mind's mental makeup and its functioning mechanisms. I was especially interested in his description of the principle behind Zen that purifies our mental makeup and assures us of absolute comfort, which is brought about through what is called 'Salvation', 'Dropping-off', or 'Enlightenment'.

By observing children, we can clearly understand the Zen's principle of acting simply. Before a child begins to speak, it really is in the state of single-mindedness. And even after learning to speak, until about the age of six or seven, they remain in the condition of "before-and-after cutoff." They simply cry, simply get angry, or simply eat as they please. Each action they do leaves little trace in their minds for long. It is impossible to anticipate what they will do next.

They cry one moment and laugh the next. They live in the world of "before-and-after cutoff." Zen is returning to this childlike world. "Before-and-after cutoff" is the principle extinguishing delusion and illuminating the mind. Children are fine models for Zen practitioners.

There were many things about Zen that were unclear to me. There were many things I wanted to know about Zen. But, the most important thing I wanted to know, was how to practice Zen in daily life after leaving the dôjô. If Zen practice had nothing to do with daily life in the regular world, this kind of Zen practice would merely be another short-lived, self-satisfying experience.

A researcher's task is to work over and through new ideas. I am constantly thinking while I work. But this kind of intellectual operation seemed to be quite the opposite of not dealing with things and leaving things just as they are. If Zen is in opposition to all kinds of intellectual activity, I wouldn't be able to accept Zen at all. This question stirred up a certain amount of doubt and anxiety in my Zen practice.

"While you are working with a computer, it is quite natural to be thinking. Even though various thoughts arise, they do not say, 'This is an arising thought.' Arising thoughts during your work are totally one with your work and the computer. When each action or activity is finished, it is over; no trace of it remains to become attached to. Thoughts and other mental activity have no true or fixed form. Thoughts originally are the natural function of

'Dropping-off'. The problem is the self that is conscious of arising thoughts. If there is no self to perceive, then thoughts are naturally cut off from before and after by activity of one's work. Therefore give yourself up to the work itself. Do you understand this point?

Worrying whether or not thoughts are arising during your work is a waste of time and creates dualistic thinking. Forget this kind of thinking and just absorb yourself in your work. Just work simply and wholeheartedly. Sometimes you have to look away from the computer screen and carefully check if you actually are functioning freely, and not attached to your work. When you are truly and simply doing the work itself, and not somehow being driven by it, then the work is doing the work. This is the form of salvation and the structure of no-self.

If there is no trace of the work in the mind after working, it means that you have worked single-mindedly and the self didn't arise in your work. Zen Master Dôgen said, 'How do you think non-thinking: thoughtless thought'. He is saying to utterly give yourself up to the activity 'as it is'.

Quickly cut off random thoughts and always return to the present moment. Because you erect the self-and-other viewpoint, things stress you. Cut off random thoughts so that the mind is no longer distracted; relax for a while, then start working again. If your single-minded devotion is strong, thoughts not related to your work drop off naturally. Don't worry about it. When doing creative work where ideas have to be worked over, fresh and free thought is necessary. This is not useless, random thinking. Utilizing this kind of thought in its most constructive way is the Dharma. When it is time to think, thinking is the Way itself.

When thinking is no longer necessary, you should return to the condition of thoughts 'before-and-after cutoff.' If before and after are not cut off from the present moment, thoughts and images continuously appear like someone forgetting to close the barn door. When the switch for turning on random thinking is on automatic, you lose control of the situation.

As your single-mindedness matures, everything naturally drops away. Right now, you only have to keep making serious efforts."

It was a great relief to hear this.

The essence of Zen is being absorbed in whatever we are doing; it has nothing to do with thinking or not thinking. When you think, you should think with your whole mind and body. What "cutting off thoughts" meant was to get rid of the habitual mind which creates the gap between us and what we are doing. We have to return to the present moment, the state of zero, after the operation of each single movement of thought is finished. The state of the mind where a single movement of thought is separate and unconnected to another is called "before-and-after cutoff." In order to maintain this condition of "before-and-after-cutoff," we have to absorb ourselves wholeheartedly in our work. In fact, we already exist in the present moment, in now, and in reality; therefore it is natural that with each passing moment past things are finished. Hearing this resolved this researcher's greatest doubt. I was greatly relieved.

A party was held at eleven o'clock after evening *zazen* in celebration of the end of my first Zen retreat.

At Shôrinkutsu anyone can have a personal interview with Rôshi at any time to inquire about the Way. Rôshi will answer a person's questions until all doubts have been resolved. And after meals he gives valuable *Dharma* talks. Both of these were a great help to me. But these little banquets also offered a valuable opportunity. It was a chance not only to be able to express our minds frankly, but also provided an atmosphere where we could listen to Rôshi's talks in a relaxed mood.

Rôshi and I were talking. His two disciples were sitting with us silently, simply listening. My questions were frank, and I asked many questions without any hesitation.

"What do you think about the understanding of Ikkyû and Ryôkan?"

"Their understanding and compassion are very deep. You should evaluate them for yourself. As a Zen practitioner, you should not judge great Zen Masters. You must respect them and learn from their contrasting styles in their effort to attain the Way.

A Zen monk of high virtue once said, 'The Zen of Ikkyû and Ryôkan is worthy of admiration, but not of learning.' You should practice hard and ascertain what he really meant by this.

There was a Zen Master in China named Gantô who was the disciple of Tokusan and the *Dharma* brother of Seppo. He was beheaded by a government official during the time when Buddhism was being suppressed in China. It was said that he cried out "Ouch!" at the moment his head was cut off. Later on, Japanese Zen Master Hakuin couldn't believe this incident. Hakuin wondered why Gantô, an Enlightened person, would cry out so shamelessly. But when Hakuin attained Great Enlightenment, he leaped for joy shouting, 'How honest Gantô is!'"

"Do you know if Hakuin's shout is the same as Gantô's?"

"At the moment Hakuin dropped off mind and body, he himself became Gantô and started dancing for joy. When the gap between mind and object disappeared, he became the object itself. He could understand Gantô totally and thoroughly.

If you forgot your doubts, you cannot distinguish clearly between truth and falseness. But Hakuin clarified his doubt with the Great Doubt. 'Ouch!' and 'How honest Gantô is!' are very much different in sound, time, meaning, and the person who uttered it. This is called distinction. But the function of selflessness without a gap works of itself. There is only that condition, and nothing else. We call this 'Equity'. The thing is the thing itself: it is 'as it is', yet it is not 'as it is'. The function of selflessness originally transcends same and different, equality and discrimination, self and other, and enlightenment and delusion. This is Salvation. The purpose of Zen Practice is to attain this for ourselves. Make no mistake of this!"

"What did Dengyo Daishi mean when he said, "Illuminate just one corner?"

"If you interpret a corner to be a tiny part of something, you misunderstand. For Dengyo Daishi, 'a part' means the universe and all things. 'Illuminate' means showing the right direction to people, in other words, presenting an ideal to people."

Rôshi answered quickly. The talk was stimulating and full of Zen spirit. It induced a pleasant sensation throughout my whole body. At that time I did not understand the profundity of his answers. But later on, as my single-minded concentration deepened, I often would catch glimpses of the meaning of what Rôshi had said. And this would always be accompanied by a faint sense of contentment. This became a wonderfully significant source of self-confidence and positive energy in my life.

This experience is characteristic of a Zen education. It differs from Japanese school education where the emphasis is on memorization. Zen is the world of realization through actual practice and cannot be attained at all through knowledge or explanation. What the practitioner is able to grasp from the teaching of the Master depends the practitioner's present capacity. The master will never attempt to force his teaching unnecessarily. Our ability to understand and grasp the teaching expands naturally as our practice deepens. The teaching is spontaneously given to hard working practitioners, but not to those whose efforts are unworthy. The law of causality is truly fair.

Realization is dependent upon one's effort. This is the essence of Zen. A striking characteristic of Zen practice is that as our practice progresses our thinking becomes more intellectual and scientific. As our mind becomes calm, our thinking becomes multifaceted, rich, and pure. For a scientist, this is extremely beneficial.

A practitioner learns how to deal appropriately with his arising emotions. His mind is calmer and is not troubled with excessive emotion.

Although Rôshi is not a scientist, his lucid analytical ability must be due to the depth of his understanding. Having come this far, I can say with more devotion and effort that I, too, could probably obtain the same capability as he.

"From now on, you will be able to understand the sutras and records of the great Zen Masters. They will become so interesting that you will not be able to stop reading them. But you shouldn't read them because it will only give you intellectual satisfaction. And it is a curse to think that you understand their meaning simply from reading them. An understanding of the sutras will not remove the gap. Understanding is of no use in actual self-cultivation.

As much as possible, refrain from stimulating the intellect. Conceptualization is like an unending, perpetual motion mechanism; it is the biggest impediment to Zen practice. The inclination to practice Zen is a product of one's disposition and the desire to seek the *Dharma*. This is the 'Way-seeking Mind.' Every person's 'Way-seeking Mind' and approach to Zen practice are different. Their ability to concentrate and their intensity of purpose are also different. Even though someone may be endowed with an excellent intellect, if his aspiration to inquire about the true self is weak, his devotion to resolve this matter will be weak.

In the end, the Mind-seeking Way is most important.

Although not a forgone conclusion, most people who come to practice Zen are highly cultured spiritually. They realize their instability and artificiality, and they want to resolve their problem. I would say that the degree of satisfaction one desires and intensity of their aspiration to attain it, along with the degree and comprehension of their own problem, are all closely related to intelligence."

Rôshi's enlightening talk continued until midnight.

He had great insight into humanity because he had closely observed (even the details of how people handled their chopsticks) from morning till night people from all walks of life in everyday lives. The weight and importance of his discernment is much different than what a scholar would learn from books. I don't think anyone else has this kind of deep understanding of humanity.

Perhaps someday a specialist of some kind with a heart and mind like Rôshi's who has devoted himself selflessly to practice Zen—even at the risk of his life—will appear and prove to be of some use in such areas as education, society, daily living, and philosophy. I would hope this would happen soon, and for the highest levels of public good.

The Ninth Day—A Terribly Big Souvenir

This was to be my final day in the dôjô. I got up at seven, cleaned my room, and washed up.

At breakfast Rôshi asked, "What is the taste of the tea [you are drinking]?

Silently and confidently I *just* drank the tea.

"You're still engaging the discriminating mind" He didn't accept my response. It was true that I had acted by means of understanding.

"You acted on pretense ruled by the intellect which understood the question and then ordered the action. As long as you keep using your head you remain in the world of delusion. You see, don't you? You still haven't become the thing itself? "You still have 40 minutes before leaving. Go sit in the zendô until then."

Just as I was about to leave for home, he gave me this terribly big souvenir.

Of course, at all times I must preserve the moment without a gap. I have to maintain the purity of my actions. In everything I do there is only endeavoring to become the thing itself.

Rôshi, his two disciples, and all the other practitioners stood by the gate and saw me off. I

bowed with my palms joined in prayer and got in a car that one of the disciples would drive taking me to the train station.

In the future, I would also be seeing other practitioners off bowing in the same manner as the car would depart and watching until the car was out of sight behind the shade of the hill. Then I would bow again deeply and quietly. This is part of the Shôrinkutsu Dôjô's Principles of Conduct.

This time my heart is full of deep emotion finding that friends in the *Dharma* see me off in the same way. But at this time, I could not really understand the undeserved reverence.

I know how important it is to treat others well, but I wonder if I actually do show the care and kindness that I should. Perhaps I really am too coarse with others. The act of truly wishing happiness for someone going home has to show in one's conduct. This is truly a prerequisite for character building. I reflected on this deeply.

But now I do see new Zen practitioners off in a spirit true to Shôrinkutsu Dôjô. It feels great. My feelings are in accord with my actions. It is both the foundation and an ideal for human beings.

Without a doubt, a gap forms when action is transmitted from mind to body. I understand intellectually what I must do, but sometimes I become impatient or irritated that I can't put it into practice. The reason for this is that the switchover process is so complicated and troublesome that it doesn't work clearly and directly. Our consideration, discrimination and random thinking interrupt the process.

The result of doing Zen practice is that the gap shrinks. After reading many *Dharma* talks and relying on personal experience, it seems that selflessness may be where mind and body become one: the gap between mind and action utterly disappears. Certainly, the *gap* itself must simply be nothing but a notion created by supposition. But as long as we hold on to such notions, it is necessary to make the effort to educate and cultivate ourselves. Zen practice is the effort to remove this *gap*. This is my conclusion from considering the mechanism of enlightenment.

As the *Shinkansen* was passing Okayama Station, I wept in sincere gratitude to Rôshi. Truly Zen practice is shedding many tears. When I arrived home, sobbing in tears of gratitude once again, I told my wife about my Zen experience.

Zen Practice Thereafter—No Need to Seek for Truth Anymore In this way I completed my first experience in Zen practice at Shôrinkutsu Dôjô; however, this did not mean at all that I realized single-mindedness. Although I sensed that I had merely taken a short glimpse into a small portion of it, there still clearly remained something unfulfilled or unsettled. After several more trips to the dôjô for Zen practice, I could finally reproduce the state in *zazen* where thoughts did not arise. After that, *zazen* became my life. And making monthly visits to the dôjô became the joy in my life. Without a doubt, one's most natural, relaxed and settled world is the realm where there is no mental surplus.

Practicing Zen in daily life was also a great problem. My work was so time consuming that I was not able to allow enough time for *zazen*. For a working person to practice Zen there is no other place to practice except in the clamorous world of appetites, loss-and-gain, and love-and-hate. But how do we temper and ripen single-mindedness in our daily lives and at work?

Although I understand how to, I sometimes found myself in helpless situations.

At times like that, my starting point for practicing Zen would begin while walking or eating.

At Shôrinkutsu, I slowed down the speed of my walking *zazen* to an extreme and concentrated on every minute movement of the muscles in the legs. At any time and any place, I tried to find a way to immediately return to the state of 'as it is'. Upon leaving the dôjô after my first experience in zazen, I forgot how to walk single-mindedly. I visited Shôrinkutsu Dôjô many times just to discover how to get it back.

Another problem was the disparity between my practice at the dôjô and my practice in daily life. Although I could continue to "knead" single-mindedness at Shôrinkutsu, I could not do it satisfactorily in daily life. Also, the disparity between *zazen* in action and in quiet sitting was another problem. I could cut off random thinking while sitting *zazen*, but I was submerged in them otherwise.

Always conscious of these circumstances, I took great pains to continue to "knead" single-mindedness. Sometimes, my aspiration (or "Way-seeking Mind") was strong and I could continue my single-minded practice at the office on the university campus. Other times, my aspiration would be weak; I would spend months wasting my time.

It is a mistake to do Zen practice in search of some outcome or result. Erecting a goal or purpose and doing *zazen* aiming for it is called "impure Zen practice." True training is single-minded sitting; it is single-minded activity. In short, it is to investigate sitting zazen 'as it is' or the activity itself, undefiled by anything. However, single-minded sitting and single-minded activity do bring about clear and affirmative effects.

I have visited Shôrinkutsu many times in the eight years since I first started practicing there.

Through continued Zen practice my character has continued to improve. This is not due to being taught by somebody, but through the continuation of single-minded practice itself. Without any blind belief in doctrine or Buddha, or in some obligation to religious faith, this higher moral character develops of itself. This is why Zen is to be the central school of Buddhism. I can testify that such things as anger, jealousy, and attachments have faded, and I have experienced an improvement in my character. My face and body remain the same; but as the habitual mind is discarded, the fluctuations in human emotions calm remarkably. Attachments to the external world have diminished, and I begin to taste the calm of composure and a presence of mind.

Man is strongly influenced by the external world through objects of sight, external circumstances, and the words of others. In particular, human beings are easily moved by the words of others. I was also one such person who was flapped like a flag by what people said.

But I cannot imagine how much I have been set free by Rôshi 's words, "Listen to what others say as you would listen to the rustling wind in the pines." Now I am fairly able to just listen when others talk.

My concentration has strengthened remarkably. Once I start to work, one or two hours pass in a twinkling. During that time, I harbor no self-consciousness. (This is the active state of selflessness. If one is totally selfless, there would be no perception of even the selflessness itself.

But because I have not penetrated my practice that far, the difference between the self and selflessness is still unclear.) The irritation and stress of my busy workload has diminished considerably.

But what is most delightful of all is that I have achieved the firm conviction that "Above and beyond this, there is no need to seek anywhere for Truth." The symptoms of that "brain ulcer" I had before practicing Zen have disappeared completely.

At the moment my eyes or ears pick up any stimulus from the external world, no thoughts arise. This is what is called the absolute present. But for a normal person, the mind is shaken by external stimulus, which sets off the process of thinking. If this didn't lead to engagement by the discriminating mind, there would be no problem. However, we ordinary humans feel such things as hatred when we see the other person and fear at the mention of death. It is due to personal views such as these that we suffer. In order to avoid such discomfort, first we must ignore those notions we raise. Then master the method of leaving objects of the external world as they are.

Finally, we must endeavor to do this constantly. The sole way to accomplish this is Zen. I have attained the means to accomplish this. But I still suffer occasionally due to my own evil feelings and wicked thoughts. Needless to say, I am not yet able to completely avoid my mental anguish. What I have reaped from my efforts in Zen practice is a grasp of a fundamental aspect of Japanese tradition. For example, my table manners naturally improved, and some bad habits I had using chopsticks disappeared spontaneously. When I drank a cup of tea I found that both my hands naturally sustained the teacup. I have rediscovered that Zen had been a foundation of traditional Japanese propriety.

Training a child to obediently answer yes is to train the child to just act simply. The scolding words of a father "Don't argue!" are clearly understandable according to the principles of Zen. A child's habit of quibbling becomes the root of future problems for the child. Unfortunately, however, we have long lost the true meaning of words like "yes" and "don't argue." Present day fathers, who just become emotional, do not know the true meaning of these words; and children reject such upbringing as outdated mores.

The meaning of the practices of other Buddhist sects became clearly understandable when measuring using the principles of Zen. Chanting the Buddha's name is one means of keeping single-mindedness. When repeatedly chanting, "*Namu* Amida Butsu," the opportunity for random thoughts to arise diminishes. The *kôan* (questions used for *zazen*) practice of "*Mu*" primarily practiced by the Rinzai school of Zen Buddhism functions the same way. The essence of chanting "*Mu*," "*Namu* Amida Butsu," or "*Namu Myôhô Renge Kyô*" are all the same.

When I look back, I find I have come to realize many things. I am relieved that my mind has become much more relaxed. However, I still have many human faults lingering and also have not yet reached the final settlement.

I resent my weak "Way-seeking Mind."

Please laugh at me.

It will only rouse me to practice again.

I have treasured the beauty of the gardens of Zen temples in Kyoto ever since first seeing them during my junior high school days. When I think about it, Zen Buddhism has added a unique quality to Japanese culture in such fields as flower arrangement, tea ceremony, calligraphy, painting gardens, cooking, etiquette, martial arts, etc. The hearts of many highly cultured people such as Sanraku Kanô, one of the most influential painters in the medieval period; Bashô Matsuo, a founder of the art of haiku; and so on, were hidden in the essence of Zen. Historical key figures such as Tokimune Hôjô, a Kamakura-shogunal regent who destroyed invading troops from the Mongol empire; Takauji Ashikaga, a founder of the Muromachi Shogunate; Munenori Yagyû, a master swordsman in the Edo period; Yoshio Ôishi, a chief retainer who sacrificed himself to revenge lord Kira who humiliated his lord Asano; Kaishû Katsu, a statesman who succeeded in changing the regime from the Tokugawa Shogunate to Meiji government in protecting Japan from the great powers of colonial rule; Takamori Saigô, a commander-in-chief of the armed force of Meiji government and so forth, trained their hearts and minds in Zen. Zen was the spiritual culture and grounding for military families and cultured people of Japan.

For the revival of this former way of life, I apply myself continuously, painstakingly, and solely to "kneading" single-mindedness.

An old road, where people of old used to trod, is now grown over because nobody walks there.

Postscript

Zen may be similar to religion in appearance, but its nature is quite different. Zen is totally distinct from such things as the occult, faith healing, superstition, gods or Buddha, or anything irrational or imperceptible. Bowing to an object of worship in a Zen temple is a way of showing respect to Buddha and his ancestors who have transmitted Zen to us. It is not due to some belief in the existence of some holy entity being present or expressed in the carved statues or painted figures.

Zen may also appear to be anti-religious, but its essence is really most religious. The fact that Zen requires no blind belief in gods or doctrine indicates an extremely anti-religious nature on one hand. But, on the other hand, because its aim is true salvation through conscious, independent, and subjective effort it possesses a most religious nature.

In the *Bendôwa* chapter of the *Shôbôgenzô* it is written, "We all are already fully endowed with the *Dharma*. However, the *Dharma* never manifests without practice, nor can it be attained without Great Awakening. The *Dharma* refers to the state of things as they are, but this state cannot be realized without undergoing Zen practice. Once you have realized this state, then you understand that *as-it-isness* is shared by all people equally.

It is written in the 56th chapter of *Lao-tsu*, "The person who knows does not speak, and the person who speaks does not know." Speaking from a Zen practitioner's point of view concerning this Taoist passage, "the person who speaks" refers to one who is only caught up in knowledge and discrimination; and "the person who knows" is the person who is comfortable in *as-it-isness*.

The expression "the person who knows does not speak" would better read "the person who knows cannot tell." It is true that *single-mindedness* and *as-it-isness* are incomprehensible. Still, Zen is not some mysterious ideology. If you study under a true Zen master, ten out of ten people will attain its essence.

The tendency in Japan is to esteem such character traits as obedience and frankness. Is it not this pure heart of *as-it-isness* itself—untainted by random, excessive, and evil thoughts, and shared equally by all human beings—which is the true religious heart of the Japanese?

It is often said that the Japanese are unreligious. There are few Japanese who could say or explain satisfactorily to other Japanese, let alone to non-Japanese, that the capacity to revere obedience and honesty is itself the religious heart of Japan. Although the Japanese don't particularly like being labeled unreligious, they can't even venture an explanation in their defense, and end up themselves wondering if perhaps it might be true. In reality, I think the Japanese do have a deeply religious heart. They only abhor dogmatic or strongly ideological religious systems.

I think the Japanese should once again realize their true religious hearts. There is no difference among nationalities or races in *as-it-isness*. In this sense Zen, being universal and international in character, is the light of hope for all mankind in this "Godless age."

I should also point that Zen is clearly different from meditation. Meditation is an act of trying to fill the heart with certain feeling of happiness. On the other hand, Zen is the act of emptying the mind and discarding everything. There is obviously a great difference between emptying the mind and filling it up with some image or feeling to attain happiness.

Zen is not a mystical spiritual experience where the unification of a divine being and man occurs. Enlightenment is empirical proof of "body and mind are one."

In short, Zen is reaching the state where action and perception become one. Furthermore, it is not attaining some supernatural power through Enlightenment. Zen is neither a concept nor a philosophy. It is action itself throughout one's whole life. Zen is a "Transmission beyond the written scriptures." It does not rely on the mere transmission of letters or words but is directly conveyed from teacher to student, from heart to heart. But it is also true that Zen makes a varied and prolific use of words. There are huge volumes of records left by the ancient Zen Masters. But no matter how much you read these records, you cannot attain Enlightenment through their study.

Ultimately Zen does not rely on words. Zen is like training someone in a sport, where the coach teaches by explaining the action in words and by showing the trainee how to move his body. Zen is mental training where, like sports training, the Zen master can only coach Zen practitioners after having seen them in action. Likewise, the principle of "a transmission outside the written scriptures" is not based on some secret doctrine. Should a Zen practitioner believe in the existence of some secret or hidden doctrine in Zen practice that hasn't yet been disclosed to him, it is only because he himself blindly chooses to believe in or imagine some grander world existing elsewhere. And when the master writes down comments to correct the practitioner's unnecessary imaginings, the practitioner yet again willfully misinterprets what the Zen master says. As long as the practitioner clings only to words, it becomes unavoidable that the master's great mercy in trying to clear up such misunderstandings only turns into a hindrance to the practitioner.

As has been indicated in the previously mentioned five items of Zen practice, the principles of Zen are concise and concrete.

Zen is not unscientific in any way. The tranquil state of mind attained through Zen practice can be demonstrated by measuring brainwaves recording the amplified recorded movement of the electric activity of the brain nerve cells. Alpha waves are produced when one is in a tranquil state. When one is practicing Zen, alpha waves are easily generated.

Zen denies neither science nor scientific knowledge. But it is the viewpoint of Zen that human beings cannot ultimately be saved by scientific knowledge. The wisdom of Zen may use scientific knowledge, but only as a means and without acquiring any dependence on it. In this way Zen is supra intellectual. In the same way, Zen utilizes logos, without becoming dependent upon it. Thus, Zen is supra logos. I would hope the reader has come to understand this from the glimpses of Rôshi 's sphere of understanding and compassion described in this book.

Zen detests understanding through knowledge. Understanding through knowledge itself, without being linked with action, is merely intellectual self-satisfaction. It is difficult to cultivate one's character only through knowledge and understanding. This is by no means an exaggeration and should be emphasized repeatedly.

There are two divergent elements coexisting in man's makeup: they are thought and action. These two are often in conflict with each another. The person inclined toward thinking does not act promptly; the person inclined toward the action does not think thoroughly enough.

It is the wise men and great pioneers of the Orient who labored trying to unify thought and action. The remarkable aspect of the Orient's traditional wisdom lies in its means to unifying these two contradictions. This method of trying to unify the two is generally referred to as moral cultivation. The unification of thought and action in the teaching of Wang Yangming (1472-1529) of China is one such example.

The special feature of the modern Japanese intellect lies in the separation of thought and action. One of the reasons for this is the Japanese educational system of post-Second World War which was predisposed with gaining knowledge. But the traditional Japanese intellect was not originally like this, especially before the Meiji era (1868-1912), and even continued after that period. For example, Rohan Kôda (1867-1947), a man of letters, wrote in his book *Theory of Effort* about his own way of moral cultivation.

A progressive international Christian scholar, Inazô Nitobe (1862-1933), wrote in *Shûyô* (Self-cultivation) the importance of "quiet thinking" and noted on "the exquisiteness of *zazen*." But as time passed, such tradition gradually lost its influence.

The current characteristics in the separation of thought and action became obvious, and acceptance of the premise of the intellect's superiority became apparent. For example, the philosopher Kiyoshi Miki (1897-1945) in his book, *Note on the Theory of Life,* said of doubt that "at the moment, the freedom of the human intellect lies in doubt...doubt purifies the human mind as a virtue of the intellect." But he also states "...in doubt there must be moderation. Only those doubts [tempered] by moderation can really be called doubt." But he never comments on the limitations of the intellect.

What I really want to stress is the almost forgotten Oriental tradition of unifying thought and action—and the restoration of it. "It" is the unification of body and mind through religious practice and the revival of moral cultivation. The modern intellects separate thought and action.

For instance, from the works of sociologist Max Weber, the modern intellect also requires a separation of scientific recognition and judgmental values. In the 20th century, the intellect had license to work self-indulgently at various levels and detached from virtue, emotion and principle. Both the magnificence and the misery of 20th century technological development were due, perhaps, to this gap between thought and action, at least from the perspective of observing the scientists themselves. In the process of the destruction of our natural and social environment, the human mind speeds toward its own ruin in alarming haste.

In the 21st century, unprecedented difficulties are expected to emerge. Will man be able to overcome these impending 21st century dilemmas with a 20th century intellect?

I am sure that the readers of this book will form various impressions of its content.

A business-person reflecting back on his life might earnestly raise the desire to enter some form of self-discipline and practice Zen for self-development.

A busy company executive may begin longing for calmness and presence of mind. An idle, young man burned out from over-indulgence goes for a midnight stroll and arrives at a turning point of his life.

An elementary school teacher portending the imminence of malevolence after observing the recurrent, unruly behavior of students at lunchtime, might somehow try to use Zen to teach ethics and morality at school.

A mother who scolds her children for every little thing might someday awaken to the flawless beauty of childhood innocence. She might also realize her calling to the noble mission of taking an active role in closely educating and nurturing the next generation.

Zen will pave the way in the frontier of neuroscience.

A neuroscientist may associate the principles of Zen with strengthening the mind's center of attention in the association area of the frontal lobe since *single-mindedness* is achieved by the arousal of attention. Regardless of our wishes, ordinary man will always be tossed about by the wind and waves in a sea of random thinking. This may be due to the wildly running speech center of the brain. It might be possible to consider Zen practice as an alternative regulator for the speech center.

A psychiatrist might become aware of the value of Morita therapy which, for example, has instructed neurosis patients to pick up cigarette butts in a nearby park. The principle behind such treatment is to control randomly dispersed thinking by having the patient concentrate on the action itself, in this case, collecting cigarette butts.

A devotee of the Chinese classics like *Confucian Analects, The Great Learning, the Doctrine of the Mean*, and *The Works of Mencius* might encounter renewed and refreshing wonder in reading them. He might say, for instance, that "the state of EQUILIBRIUM" which is defined in *The Doctrine of the Mean* as "the mind while there are no stirrings of pleasure, anger, sorrow, or joy" means *single-mindedness* itself.

Here at the doorstep of the 21st century where man is about to encounter many unprecedented problems, a philosopher might pay more serious attention to the significance of ancient Oriental thought and ideas, like the Japanese philosopher Kitarô Nishida who confronted dualism with the help of Zen.

I have nearly finished writing a report on the 2,500-year-old secret of Zen.

There may be some readers who think they have now "understood" Zen by reading this book. This is the typical attitude of intellectual understanding. It is impossible to explain sweetness to those who have never tasted sugar, nor Zen to those who have never experienced it. A man knows what *hot* is by touching hot water for the first time. Zen is the world where cool is cool, and hot is hot. If you want to know what Zen is, you have to go to a *dôjô* to practice Zen under a true Zen master. Practicing Zen under a true master is everything!

I hope many people will practice Zen under a true master and that Zen will become the household medicine for everyone. Zen practice is only effective under a true Zen master. It is useless under a master who has not genuinely attained the Way for himself.

Scientific investigation of the mechanisms of Zen is of secondary importance. It should be emphasized that scientific understanding never saved man from his fundamental suffering.

However, scientific investigation could shed light on the mental makeup of man in turmoil. The scientists who want to study Zen scientifically should reach at least the stage of *methodless-method*, which needs vigorous practice of at least three years to attain. Otherwise, the scientist will not know what Zen is; and, more distressfully, his superficial understanding becomes a basis for subsequent, misguided scientific investigation.

Methodless-method is the ultimate way of Zen practice. It is conducted without the mind utilizing any method or means. In other words, no-method is the true method of genuine Zen practice. To reach this stage without needless delay, you must keep your mind at the point of each present action— something that is changing each moment.

A Zen practitioner must pay careful attention to the real and tangible, phenomenal world of the present moment; for instance, to the bottom of your foot while walking, or your tongue or the touch of tableware while eating.

Zen practice is an effort to concentrate one's mind completely on the point which is changing every moment. To reach what is called the *methodless-method*, a Zen practitioner has not only to cut off any thoughts and images that arise suddenly and unexpectedly, but also transcend all delusion and personal views, which are deeply rooted in the mind. Such delusions and personal views are the source of the mind's strongest attachments and are the most difficult mental habits to eliminate.

As we first embark on Zen practice we almost always give in to our deeply-rooted delusions and personal views. However, these are the very enemies or demons we must overcome. Zen practice is to keep fighting them, however hard it may be, without giving up. Man willfully creates his own delusions and personal views, and becomes attached to them. Attachment leads to emotional stimulation, which sometimes—depending on circumstances— leads to emotional outbreaks. One method of Zen practice has the Zen practitioner cut such emotions off by asking deeply within himself, "Where does this thing come from?" The Zen practitioner should continue this battle until the emotion is cut off at the root whenever and no matter how often the emotion arises. There is no other way to overcome emotions than cutting them off completely. There is nobody other than you yourself who can dispose of delusions and personal views because it is you yourself who has created them. Your difficulties in overcoming delusion will be indescribable.

Seeking understanding from others will be impossible because others will not be able to understand even if you try to explain. Will your aspiration to seek the Way win? Or will the negligent mind triumph?

When your emotions explode, they become violent passion. They cannot be instantly calmed.

We are carried away by them. However, the Zen practitioner moves the battle line forward to the point before the eruption by perceiving the awakening of their initial stirrings in the mind, then immediately cuts off any thoughts or emotions right after they first originate. In other words, he reaches the mental state where the first thought does not trigger a second—only a single action takes place instead of chain reaction. He comes to realize that preparation for conflict in peacetime is much more effective than engaging the enemy after being harassed. At this stage of Zen practice the fear of phenomena such as emotional outbursts that grow and burn out of control rapidly disappears, and the emotions cease from becoming problematic at all. This is what is called salvation through Zen practice or the transformation in mental structure.

Reaching the stage of *methodless-method* is the juncture for Zen practice to take root in the daily life. If a practitioner is not able to reach this stage, his or her practice ends up, sooner or later, merely as a temporary experience without the capacity for salvation. It would be no exaggeration to say that everything said about Zen by a person who has never reached the stage of *methodless-method* is complete delusion and personal opinion. If you can come to the stage of *methodless-method*, your "Way-seeking Mind" endeavoring to live every day in the Way has strengthened as much as your delusive mind has weakened.

Arriving at the *methodless-method* depends upon the strong will to transcend oneself and the effort to accomplish one's ideal. In short, it depends on the quality of the vessel. Depending on wholehearted and extreme effort, one can attain the capacity to dwell in the present moment where one can clearly see the arising point which cultivates all random thinking and emotions.

While a practitioner is still using *zazen* as a means or method, he or she differentiates *zazen* and their present reality. This distinction is a hindrance to practice. One must realize that all of our functions themselves always have been the Way from the beginning. Realizing this, the practitioner discovers that in both quiet sitting and in daily life any method or means separate from the present moment is unnecessary. Thereafter, the practitioner's approach of the necessity of utilizing a method or means for practice changes. This is *methodless-method*. Reaching *methodless-method* he or she becomes able to deepen *single-mindedness* at any time and place,

and in direct response to the thing itself. It means that they have attained the ability to give themselves up to the thing itself becoming intimate, or one, with it. From this time on, they enjoy the capacity to walk in the Way. *Methodless-method* requires extreme efforts to reach. Such effort may appear odd or strange to people. The practitioner may sit in his room avoiding conversation with family. He may avoid watching TV and listening to music. Perhaps he will eat silently with a grave, aloof, and expressionless look. But through such strenuous efforts in keeping *single-mindedness*, one can preserve *methodless-method*. At times like these, one can recall and acutely understand the words of Lao Tzu who said, "When superior leaders hear of the Tao, they diligently try to practice it. When average leaders hear of the Tao, they appear both aware and unaware of it. When inferior leaders hear of the Tao, they roar with laughter. Without sufficient laughter, it could not be the Tao."

Afterword

I regret that I started practicing Zen at the late age of 42. It is shameful that I am slow in progressing.

It is said that if you want to examine a Zen practitioner, take a look at his or her daily action. If a penetrating Zen master would inspect these writings in light of my daily actions, he would think them quite absurd. My writing cannot avoid the intellectual understanding that I myself refute in the book. The essence of Zen practice is private and personal—a practitioner seeks his master's inspection continuously, while he holds the 'true mind' privately and honestly.

Moreover, one who has not become enlightened should never talk about Zen because it disgraces the *Dharma* by disseminating incorrect teaching.

However, this book is prepared as an introduction to Zen practice by permission of Kido Rôshi to provide some information about Zen as it should be and let people know the importance of practicing Zen under the guidance of a true Zen master. Because of the immaturity of my own Zen practice, I sincerely hope that the true value and significance of Zen would not be mistakenly passed down through my writings.

One starts Zen practice by his 20s, he or she will become a great being as the ancient great Zen Masters.

One commences to practice Zen in his 30s, he or she will be the best professional of his field. One begins Zen practice in his 40s, he or she will be a good professional and parent.

One meets Zen in his 50s, he or she will attain peace of mind.

Atsunobu Tomomatsu
January 1998.

APPENDIX

...

PROCESS OF ZEN PRACTICE

• • •

Kido Inoue Rôshi explains the process of Zen practice, including the stage of methodless-method, [See (6) and (7)] as follows:

There are several essential points in the process of Zen practice. As stages do not exist originally, this list of stages is not definitive and is only for the sake of reference. It is nothing more. This is because everyone's condition is different. But, practically speaking, from the teacher's standpoint this seems to be how a practitioner's mental structure is transformed.

(1) Enlightenment means attaining the Mind of Shakyamuni and mastering the *Buddha-Dharma*. In order to attain it, you must: throw away all greed; vow to all Buddhas and gods your aspiration to attain the True Way; show deep reverence and esteem for the ancient great Zen Masters; and seek a true teacher.

(2) When you find a true teacher, simply believe in his teaching and practice accordingly.

(3) Be attentive of the self in the present moment and throw away random thinking. Continue doing this without interruption. But because the power of the *habitual mind* is immense, you instantly lose the present moment. Here you must redouble your efforts. Practice can become very difficult at these times.

(4) In order to cut off random thinking and to force yourself to return to the present moment, turn your upper body from side to side after each single breath. This will also prevent physical stiffness and improve the smooth flow of both body and mind. This is also an excellent method to prevent drowsiness.

(5) As you come to distinguish the real moment from momentarily arising thoughts, less strain will be needed to return to your present self. At this point

149

your suffering and anguish will diminish, the boundary between reality and thought will become clearer, and doing *zazen* will at once become easier.

(6) In due time, scattered thinking will subside. You will no longer be led around by random thoughts. You will be able to let them alone by ignoring them. At this point in your practice you will be able to quickly perceive the instant when thoughts, conception, and consciousness arise. And you will come to realize the world where thoughts are cut off. This is the world of emptiness. Here is where *zazen* becomes extraordinarily interesting. You will gain the ability of continuously perceiving the overall moment-to-moment movements in your daily life. The mind ceases to move toward delusion. But because random thoughts still continue to flicker tempting you to give in sometimes, you must continually be on guard that the mind is not distracted.

(7) Then you reach the point of pure thoughtless-thought, cut off from before and after. You come to realize your original nature confirming there is no need for any method or approach needed in practicing Zen. Taking an approach to do something defiles the world 'as it is'. You only need to be just as you are, leaving yourself to the world of serene wholeness in absolute uniformity. After that, you only have to penetrate. True Zen practice is simply the present moment, and nothing else. There is just each moment. The serenity one experiences is an emotional calm that appears strange or abnormal to others. One realizes that one already conducts his life in Buddha Nature; *simply* seeing, hearing, feeling, and thinking as these functions operate on their own. One consents to the state of things as they are, preceding words and concepts. Various doubts melt away. Because you have gained an understanding of the writings of the ancient great Zen Masters, intellectual stimulation becomes fascinating. But it is still best to avoid reading them.

(8) Truly and incisively penetrating the thing itself, one plunges into selflessness. This is the reward of emptiness. It is a moment of great joy. When the *gap* collapses, it becomes clear that the *gap* itself was just an illusion. This is Enlightenment and Nirvana. It is the true present. It is the world where the past drops off and *concerns* no longer arise. We become the free functioning of all our endowed faculties. They simply operate according to cause and effect. The mind, too, functions instantaneously according to the circumstances of the present, so we cannot find any place where the mind is. This is what manifests the moment the *gap* disappears. The glad tidings of "Form is emptiness; emptiness is form." is conveyed to you, and you truly understand what *single-mindedness* is. From then on, even in the mundane world you never lose the present moment and are able to act *simply* as all your endowed faculties operate naturally. But still the ego-self remains to occasionally arise.

(9) From this time on, one enters post-Enlightenment practice. Awakening itself brings enormous conviction and strength, which conversely stands before us blocking the Way to perfect liberation. Post-Enlightenment practice is casting off even Enlightenment itself. Since originally absolutely nothing exists, perceiving Enlightenment itself is also delusion. If we possess nothing, it is possible to become anything according to circumstances. This is called true liberation or freedom. The way to discard Enlightenment is by acting *simply* (*single-mindedly*). Throwing away even the *Buddha-Dharma*, Enlightenment, and Buddha, we simply "knead" the present moment by becoming pure function 'as it is'. Like a rail stretching ten thousand miles, one must penetrate simply and solely into *single-mindedness*. Then through *single-mindedness*, *single-mindedness* consumes itself. It is essential for practitioners to keep on preserving the present moment without being neglectful for even a moment in making reference to the records of the ancient great Zen Masters and the Masters themselves.

(10) The crowning accomplishment of throwing away both Enlightenment and the *Buddha-Dharma* is Great Enlightenment. In True Reality there is neither what is considered reality nor what is not considered reality. This is the same illuminating world of our great compassionate teacher Shakyamuni Buddha who declared upon awakening, "In all of heaven and earth, I alone am the World-honored One." A man of Great Enlightenment engages in his entire life and death in joy and dignity by giving himself up to the everlasting profoundness of existence; and empowered with boundless confidence and peace of mind saves others and the world.

National Teacher Daito (1282-1337), Myôchô Sôhô left a verse as his last words:

> *Cutting the great Zen Masters into half—*
> *Polishing a razor-sharp sword all the time;*
> *Where utterly inexpressible in words*
> *Fangs bite the empty sky.*

Even at this point, the past great Zen Masters endeavored all the more to "knead" single-mindedness. They have exhausted Enlightenment they still continue to polish the world where there is nothing to polish. They had nothing to say, so words were thrown away, and they would not even open their mouths. Not even Buddha could disturb them. Buddha probably bowed his head to them in deep gratitude. True endeavor must be accompanied by a magnificent setting. This is because results befittingly accompany their causes. Because of the very fact that the ancient great Masters left us the sacred teaching, it is possible through endeavor for anyone to accomplish the Way today. The *Buddha-Dharma* penetrating *Buddha-Dharma*, Truth fostering Truth, and Mind penetrating Mind are all due to the Way. Therefore we practice the Way for the sake of the Way. This is the Mind that seeks the Way. Man is a creature who, above all, loves and values Truth. Through repentance he has the endowed capacity to readily transform himself. Through this capacity and the power of his ideals, man maintains a firm belief in the unfathomable preciousness of this existence. Man's center will always be his spirit and heart. And the core of this is the *true mind*, a desire for self-improvement, and compassion. It is also ideals, endurance, introspection, and repentance. This is the mind void of deceit and betrayal. It is the sanctity that values above all the Great Way that leads there.

It is said that time flies swifter than an arrow, and one's fate strikes quicker than lightning.

Likewise, the ancient great Zen Master cried out, "Others are not me. There is no time to wait."

Let us value and preserve these words. We should hasten to actually resurrect the ancient Masters.

ACKNOWLEDGEMENT

• • •

I would like to heartily thank Mr. Dôiku Griffin, Ms. Florence In-Holsang, Mr. Tadaaki Komori, Mr. Osamu Takamiya, Mr. Hisanori Kaneyama, Mr. Sigetsune Yamoto, and Ms. Miyuki Ortiz-Rivera, who, in spite of their very busy daily lives, have voluntarily contributed their time and effort to translation of this book. They are my true fellow Zen practitioners who think more of the Way than anything else. I would also thank Ms. Lori Ann Desrosiers and Ms. Kelly Nishimura for proofreading this manuscript.

GLOSSARY

...

Many different words are used to explain the absolute present: *shikan (single-mindedness), samadhi, absorption, true mind, Now, before-and-after-cutoff,* etc. All of these point to the reality of the present moment. Although nuances may subtly differ, all of these point from different perspectives to the absolute present. They should be understood as essentially the same.

Absorption (Zenjô): The unified mind undivided by thoughts or notions.

Awakening Synonymous with Satori: Enlightenment and **Dropping-off**. See **Satori**.

Before-and-after-cutoff (Zengo Saidan): The state of mind in which the arising of a thought (*before*) and its cessation (*after*) are clearly recognized.

Buddha-Dharma (Buppô): The teaching Shakyamuni Buddha expounded as a result of his Awakening that the true nature of all things is constantly changing (transient), is without beginning or end (selfless), and cannot be perceived (formless).

Concerns (kodawari): Not only something that worries you, such as the terror of death, but also a discriminatory thought, such as a personal view, a fixed idea, a prejudice, etc. As the product from discriminatory thinking, you may often overlook such *concerns* since the products themselves blind you; or, you misinterpret them as being your opinions and therefore an essential part of your identity. Similar to the *habitual mind.*

Dharma (or Ho): The provisional name given to the way things are as they are, i.e., sugar is sweet, salt is salty, etc. It is also used synonymously with *Buddha-Dharma.*

Dôjô: A place for training

Dokusan (doku: alone, san: to go to the teacher to inquire): Having personal interviews with the Master to inquire about the *Dharma*. This includes inquiring about one's Zen practice in dealing with various problems or doubts encountered in one's practice. It is also an opportunity for the Master to take a look into the mental state and method of practice of the practitioner.

Dropping-off (Datsuraku): Synonymous with Satori, Enlightenment, and Awakening. See Satori.

Enlightenment: Synonymous with Satori, Awakening, and Dropping-off.

Habitual mind (kokoro no kuse): Similar to *concerns*.

Heart Sutra (*Hannya-shingyo*): One of the most important sutras in Mahayana Buddhism and particularly emphasized in Zen. It expounds in a clear and concise manner the teaching of emptiness.

Hippocampus: A small region deep in each temporal lobe. It plays a major role in laying down memory traces.

Kenshô: To realize Buddha-nature. It is originally synonymous with Enlightenment, however, it is treated as the beginning of true training in *kôan* Zen investigating old standard (*kosoku*) *kôan*.

Kinhin: Single-minded walking in the zendô

Kôan: Questions used for Zen practice. There are two types of *kôan*: an old standard *kôan* (*kosoku kôan*) and an actual *kôan* (*genjo kôan*). An old standard *kôan*, which is usually taken from ancient collections of Zen *kôan* like *Mumonkan* and *Hekiganroku*, cannot be solved rationally. The practitioner is obliged to "hold" the *kôan* constantly in mind, day and night. Concentration increases until the tension causes rational thinking to give way under the pressure and a breakthrough occurs. Some Great Zen masters warned that these *kôan* were misused by mistaken or pretended Zen masters. An actual *kôan*, for example, "What is 'This Taste'?" "What is 'This Thing'?" "Who is 'This Person' listening to the sound?" and so on, is used to become the activity or the thing itself.

Kyôgai: The scope of the mind's eye to discern human nature and to influence people through its virtuous power; i.e., one's sphere of understanding of human nature and compassion toward other human beings.

Methodless-method (kufû naki kufû): Advanced Zen practice free from any fixed methods, with little consciousness of one's doing practice.

Mistaken Zen master (jashi): a Zen master who believes that he has experienced Enlightenment, mistakenly assuming some unusual experience such as *makyô* (abnormal but harmless visual sensations which most beginners experience in *zazen* practice) to be an Enlightenment experience or mistaking half-baked *kôan Kenshô* as Enlightenment. These kinds of mistaken Enlightenment are called *kanjô zatori* —emotional "Enlightenment."

Now (Ima): Synonymous with the absolute present and *sokkon*. See *sokkon*.

Polarizing fatigue (katayori hirô): Fatigue naturally arising locally, for instance, in the shoulder, back, waist, foot, or knee, from the strain of sitting for a long time.

Post-Enlightenment practice (gogo no shugyô): Practice of throwing away Enlightenment to attain Great Enlightenment (*Daigo*).

Rôshi: Traditionally, a title given to an enlightened Zen master (*rô*: old and excellent, *shi*: teacher). In present-day Japan, however, Zen priests are often addressed as "Rôshi" merely out of respect for their position and age.

Rôni: A title given to an old virtuous nun (*rô*: old and excellent, *ni*: nun).

Samadhi (zanmai): The condition where the mind is occupied only by the functioning senses—a state free of conception and miscellaneous thought.

Satori: Synonymous with Enlightenment, Dropping-off or Awakening. An experience which, in most cases, is characterized by suddenness after a long search, an instantaneous and spontaneous realization of the oneness of the whole universe, accompanied by a great peace of mind and satisfaction in this total unity or oneness. A practitioner eager for Satori but unsupervised by a true Zen master may mistake certain illusions or sensations for Enlightenment. The only person who can lead practitioners along the right path to Enlightenment and judge the authenticity of the Satori experience is a true Zen master who himself has experienced genuine Satori under a true teacher. Here lies the importance of the Dharma line of transmission that has been handed down from master to master.

Shikan: Synonymous with single-mindedness. See single-mindedness.

Single-mindedness (shikan): Sole activity 'as it is' at the absolute present where no thoughts intervene. Single-minded breathing is, for instance, the state where the breathing itself is doing the breathing, with no thoughts intervening. See Shikan.

Sokkon: Synonymous with the absolute present and *Now*. The state of mind where random thoughts no longer arise. It is the world 'as it is': just as one sees, hears, and experiences without the intervention of thought, discrimination, or consideration of any kind.

True Zen master (shôshi): Zen master who has experienced Enlightenment and knows the right way to Enlightenment.

Thalamus: The deeper nuclear structures positioned behind the basal ganglia and medial to them. They serve largely to integrate sensory and ever more refined messages at a subcortical level. They are also engaged in complex interactions with the cortex.

True mind (shônen): The mind without thought; or, the state of thoughtless thought

Zazen: Traditionally and formally means single-minded sitting in the lotus posture in the zendô. However, at Shôrinkutsu *Dôjô* practitioners, although encouraged to sit in the traditional lotus posture, are permitted to sit in any comfortable posture. Beginners are advised to turn their upper body from side to side each time they breathe in order to stop thinking randomly and prevent *polarizing* fatigue which reduces the efficiency of *zazen*. zendô A hall in which to practice *zazen*

AUTHOR'S PROFILE

• • •

Atsunobu Tomomatsu, Ph.D. is a professor at Utsunomiya University, Utsunomiya, Tochigi Prefecture, Japan. He currently maintains this position specializing in international development cooperation for developing countries (See *Who's Who in the World 2003*, Marquis Who's Who, New York). He was born in 1948 and spent his childhood in Nagoya. He majored in biochemistry at Saitama University, Urawa, Saitama Prefecture and agricultural chemistry at the graduate school of Nagoya University. He has previously held positions with: Bogor Agricultural University in Indonesia, 1980-83, as a technical cooperation expert; The Japan International Cooperation Agency, 1983-1991, as a development specialist; and The International Food Policy Research Institute in USA, 1986-88, as a visiting research fellow. Since beginning his Zen practice under Kido Inoue Rôshi in 1990, he regularly spends time at Shôrinkutsu *Dôjô*, Takehara, Hiroshima Prefecture for the purpose of attaining Enlightenment

EPILOGUE

• • •

- Awakening to the Ultimate Truth -

Kido Inoue

There is always an effective approach to any practice, which makes it more accessible and definitely rewards the effort made to achieve the goal within a relatively short span of time. Zen practice is no exception. To awaken in Zen practice, you need to calm your scattering mind, cut off your random thoughts and continually return to the single-pointedness of the present. This is how Zen practice starts. Naturally the process varies, each individual reflecting the differences in perseverance, faith and concentration. And similarly, any difficulties depend on the various habits each individual has formed. But once the false boundary of the separate-self disappears, everyone seems to exhibit the same characteristic - a mind of clarity, simplicity and openness.

The crucial requirement is to thoroughly investigate your mind until the fundamental great doubt arises. You must avoid being complacent with your small successes. And you must refrain from any temptation to arbitrarily attach your own definition to the Dharma, enlightenment or Zen.

The two most important approaches to Zen practice are first, just sit, and second, ask your teacher about the Dharma in detail. Listen to what is said, work over it, and revise and improve on your understanding; then have your teacher check your understanding. If any doubts remain, then be sure to ask further questions so you can confirm your understanding of the Dharma. When you feel confident about your understanding, then without a particle of doubt, apply the teachings to consistent practice.

The following ten steps are a rough sequence of spiritual unfolding in

Zen practice with the caveat that the process varies with every individual and that the mind may or may not undergo this sequential transformation. But my teaching experience seems to suggest that transformative process follow a certain sequence. So I present them as a reference.

1. Enlightenment is about the spirit of the Buddha, realized as your spirit - the embodiment of the Dharma as your life experience. To do Zen practice, abandon your distracting desires. Vow resolutely to the buddhas and to yourself to attain the Way. Show great reverence and affection to all the past teachers and strive to find the right teacher.

2. When you meet the right teacher, have faith in what they teach and solely put it into practice.

3. When doing zazen, continuously cut off random thoughts, observe and sustain your focus on each single breath. Each breath is the self in the present moment. The habitual patterning of your mind still holds a tight grip, and you tend to lose sight of your present self very quickly. This is the time you need to apply effort above and beyond the power of acquired habits. Doing this can be most excruciating.

4. After each breath, twist your body gently once left and right. This helps to get rid of random thoughts, relieves stiffness, improves the energy flow of both body and mind, and arrests sleepiness in sitting.

5. When you begin to differentiate moments of thinking and the reality of what is right now, it becomes easier to bring yourself back to the present. Strain is no longer necessary. Any suffering in sitting ceases. Seeing the border between the real world and thoughts, zazen instantly turns into enjoyable experience.

6. Before long, your scattering mind calms down. You are not taken by thoughts even if they arise, leaving them as they are. Around this time, you can trace the instant when thoughts and consciousness begin to rise. Then you begin to see the source itself of cutting off thoughts, where nothing exists. Zazen becomes inspiring. And it is possible to be clearly conscious of each moment throughout your daily activities. Your mind is no longer easily distracted. But it is still necessary to remain on guard, not allowing your mind to be stolen by senses and perceptions, because random thoughts do continue to rise.

7. Then you attain thoughtless thought - the realm of no before and after. You begin to appreciate your original nature, confirming that you must do absolutely nothing. If you do, you know it is driven by an ego-self, thus defiling the Dharma. It is the realm of suchness, the union with the Original Self. You are simply that awareness, resting in serenity. From here, you merely penetrate. Authentic practice is just the present moment. Your emotion quieten and you abide in profound tranquility. It is the realm of the

senses and perceptions as they are. You understand what enlightenment is, what your present reality prior to thoughts and words is. All doubt disappears. The teachings of the past masters appear strikingly clear. Unaware, this can stimulate your intellectual satisfaction, therefore reading needs to be avoided at this stage.

8. You penetrate the reality of life, plunge into selflessness and reach emptiness. It is a moment of exhilaration. With the false boundary disappearing, you now realize the separation itself was imaginary. This is Nirvana and enlightenment - being wholly in the present where the past has fallen away. You are free from any anxiety or preoccupation. This is the realm in which all the faculties you are naturally endowed with simply function according to conditions and circumstances. Because your mind is operating in response to conditions of the immediate and utter present, there is nothing that exists. It is a decisive insight. You are just this; you experience the message of 'Form is emptiness; emptiness is form'. The true meaning of 'as-it-is' becomes yours. For the first time you can live out of your Original Self without any need to be otherwise. You have direct access to your Original Self, free from ego. But you need to remain vigilant; there are still remnants of ego rising like small flame out of ashes.

9. Now begins practice after enlightenment. With enlightenment itself comes exceptional conviction and strength. However, acknowledging enlightenment becomes a hindrance. Now is the practice of letting go even enlightenment. Whether thoughts or enlightenment, if you perceive and own them, both turn into delusion. If there is nothing to hold onto, you can become anything according to life circumstances. That is true freedom. The knack of letting go of even enlightenment is, whatever you do, just do it. You practise letting everything go, be it the Dharma, enlightenment or Buddha. You transcend the awareness of just doing by just doing. Endeavour to dwell in the present without ever backsliding.

10. When you let go of enlightenment and the Dharma, you attain the great accomplishment: Great Enlightenment. Great Truth is void of what is labelled truth and not truth. Here you reach the realm of spiritual development equal to Shakyamuni Buddha, the world of "In all of heaven and earth, I alone am the world-honored one." You illuminate the world; you live and die willingly and with dignity, surrendering yourself to be part of the eternal flow of life. Empowered with boundless faith and peace of mind, you save people and the world. National Teacher Daito said, "Having achieved the Great Enlightenment, I transcend the Buddha and patriarchs and continue my practice to become this moment." Profoundly enlightened, he utterly threw that away, too, and continually refined where there was nothing more to refine. Going beyond words, he forgot about words and never opened his

mouth. Not even Buddha himself could find him. But, for sure, Buddha honored him.

The beauty and power of the Way always unfolds with true endeavor. This is because results befittingly accompany their causal actions. For as much as the revered teachings of old masters do exist, anyone who practices them can be saved. The Dharma permeating the Dharma, truth fostering truth, mind penetrating mind: all is the Way. Thus, we practice the Way for the sake of the Way. This is Bodaishin, the mind that seeks the Way.

Human being love and value truth above anything else. Every human life is utterly sacred, and this sanctity lies in our inherent capacity for repentance and transformation. Core of our being is, in all respects, in our mind and spirit, which, in turn, finds its center in the True Mind, the mind of aspiration and compassion, together with self-reflection, repentance, vision and perseverance. It is a mind free of deception and betrayal, possessing the dignity which values, above all, the Dharma. Together with the people from all over the world, I earnestly pray for the peace and well-being of our future generations.

More than any other time in history, I am reminded of the pleas of the patriarch: "Fate strikes like lightning, time passes quicker than an arrow." And his encouraging words for all of us: "Others are not me. Do not wait."

Time is urgently calling for the rebirth of the patriarchs.

Where are such persons?

ZAZEN - THE WAY TO AWAKENING

• • •

GLOSSARY OF ZEN BUDDHIST TERMS

bodai-shin; way-seeking mind, the mind aspiring toward enlightenment

dokusan; personal interview with the Roshi

Dharma; the way, the ultimate truth, the teaching of the Buddha

innen-muryo; an innumerable succession of incidents taking place, depending on countless direct and indirect causes

jita-ichinyo; unity of self and others

kaatz; a great shout transcending words and concepts used by Zen masters to wake people up from delusions and attachment

ku; the original unity of self and others, emptiness

kyousaku; wake up stick used to encourage Zen students

mondo; dialogue between Roshi and student/s

mu; literally 'no-thing'

mumyo; literally the absence of light; the world of spiritual ignorance, suffering, delusions and attachments

Prajina Paramita; lit. 'perfection of wisdom'; term for Mahayana sutras, the essence of which is chanted daily in Zen temples

roshi; Zen Master, literally 'venerable teacher'

samadhi; profound peace, stillness of mind

samu; work practice around zendo

satori; the experience or condition of enlightenment

sesshin; Zen Buddhist retreat of 5 to 7 days

shikan; lit, 'nothing but', single-minded concentration in the present moment

tada; things just as they are

wabi, sabi; elegant mature simplicity

zazen; seated, focused meditation, formal Zen Buddhist practice

zendo; Zen hall, Zen Buddhist centre

CONTACT ADDRESS

• • •

Shorinkutu Dojo, 2-10-1 Tadanoumi-tokonoura
Takehara-shi Hiroshimaken, zip 729-2314, Japan
Tel. 81-846-26-1264
Fax. 81-846-26-0565
URL: http://www.geocities.jp/shorinkutu/
E-mail: shorinkutu@ybb.ne.jp

KIDO INOUE was born in 1940; he took his first religious vows at thirteen. In 1962, he received a bachelor of arts degree in Oriental Philosophy at Aichi University. In 1981, he was appointed to be head priest of Kaizoji; in 1984, he became the Fifth Abbot of Shorinkutsu Seminary. This is his first book to be published in English translation.